Hidden America

The Spiritual Legacy of the Founding Fathers And the Nation's Native Ancestors

Luigi Morelli

Cover Art by Barton Landfair and Sue Fullam

National Library of Canada Cataloguing in Publication

Morelli, Luigi, 1958-
Hidden America : spiritual forces at the birth of a nation / Luigi Morelli.

Includes bibliographical references.
ISBN 1-55395-414-9

I. Title.

E169.12.M67 2003 973 C2002905810-4

TRAFFORD

This book was published *on-demand* in cooperation with Trafford Publishing.
On-demand publishing is a unique process and service of making a book available for retail sale to the public taking advantage of on-demand manufacturing and Internet marketing. **On-demand publishing** includes promotions, retail sales, manufacturing, order fulfilment, accounting and collecting royalties on behalf of the author.

Suite 6E, 2333 Government St., Victoria, B.C. V8T 4P4, CANADA
Phone 250-383-6864 Toll-free 1-888-232-4444 (Canada & US)
Fax 250-383-6804 E-mail sales@trafford.com
Web site www.trafford.com TRAFFORD PUBLISHING IS A DIVISION OF TRAFFORD HOLDINGS LTD.
Trafford Catalogue #02-1129 www.trafford.com/robots/02-1129.html

10 9 8 7 6 5 4

CONTENTS

Acknowledgements

This book would not have been possible without the help of a few devoted friends. Most of all I wish to thank Joyce who edited the numerous drafts leading to the final version. She gave me much useful feedback and continued support. I owe to Bruce a dispassionate analysis of my initial effort that helped me mature my thoughts and evolve the style. I am also grateful to Emory for editing my second draft and giving many useful suggestions. Other friends have at different times read and given input about different parts of the work. Among them I am indebted to R. H., Stephen and Malcolm.

Introduction

Three Holidays and the American Dream

"... what is meant if, as is frequently done, one speaks of the "American dream?" It is the feeling that something was at work at the founding of America that was "not of this world", something that arose out of primal creative dreams of the world, out of forces of the world, out of forces working unbeknown to human beings. A creative dream can rise up at any time in suitable individuals, and has indeed emerged in them."

(The Other America, Carl Stegmann)

The three holidays we will examine in this essay revolve around or reflect back upon the history of the founding of the nation. This work has tried to give some names to the sources of this creative dream, as well as to the dreamers who promoted it.

The part of American history, myth and legend explored here revolves around the time of the colonies and the foundation of the new nation. While looking at it from different perspectives, a theme emerged that links the different and separate strands into a unity. It is what I called 'the American holidays'. It would be hard to define which holidays are truly American, and which ones are only American. Are Labor Day or Columbus Day uniquely American festivals? Only to a degree. Nevertheless the festivals here considered are mostly without an equivalent elsewhere, with the exception of Thanksgiving, which is also celebrated in Canada.

This work will consider three current American holidays, and a fourth no longer celebrated. Paramount to our understanding is the historical or symbolic setting they commemorate, as well as how the holiday itself evolved. This will be the first lens under which they will be viewed. Furthermore, the holidays naturally evolve to a stage where images are given form, be they myths, legends, or idealized pictures of an actual historical reality. It is the purpose of this work to understand what the images want to tell us not only about the holidays but also about the American psyche. Since part of this reservoir of images actually concerns historical individuals, I have addressed aspects of biography, in order to better discern life patterns, trends and links of destiny. We will see that history, legend and myth or the images that develop from a biography mutually reinforce each other. In fact this way of looking at the holidays is an artistic complement to the scientific approach of history. It allows us to penetrate the American soul, a reality that we may sense to a degree but can only describe by analogies.

The holidays and celebrations of a young nation such as the United States are likely to bear a mix of political, patriotic and spiritual overtones. We will look at patriotic and political ideas only where they constitute an obvious precedent and break from the past. What matters most are the conditions that brought these changes into being, and what was unique about their evolution. The Fourth of July will absorb much of our attention, because it is the most significant turning point in the nation's history.

As might be expected, a theme will emerge constantly: the interaction between Native and European cultures at work in the North American continent. We will try to place these influences in time, characterize them and show how they mutually enrich each other. In this process, much will appear that may seem surprising or little known about American history. With this in mind it must be underlined that this work is merely a beginning that owes much to the dedicated work of many researchers or historians who have not received the recognition they deserve for truly ground-breaking work. I have felt the need to carefully document much of my research where facts are not widely known, hence the numerous references. Most of the topics treated are not found in standard history textbooks.

To link the holidays together two small chapters are included, which examine the evolution of religious and spiritual ideas during the 18th and 19th centuries respectively. My aim is to enable the reader to better place the festivals in the context of the times. These chapters also serve the purpose of illustrating how the social-political striving of the country evolved in relation to the religious-spiritual pursuits of the times. The interaction should highlight what is peculiar to America in this relationship, particularly in contrast with England and France, the two countries that had a major role and influence in the affairs of the new nation.

Finally we will look at the future of the three holidays envisioned. All the spiritual influences which brought them to birth have lost their impetus, witness the holidays' frequent lack of life and vibrancy. However, new ideas and new forces are coming to the surface. We will try to identify in which direction they point, and to where the American Dream may be moving.

Chapter 1

The Role of Religion in the 18th Century

"(In America) you would meet a politician where you would expect to find a priest"

(Democracy in America: Alexis de Tocqueville)

In order to examine the origins of the major American holidays, we will need to understand the religious atmosphere of the eighteenth century. This will especially help us to understand the influences behind Independence Day, as well as those behind the forgotten holiday of Saint Tammany. In these two holidays we can see the relationships between religious and social-political thinking. The above observation of de Tocqueville strikes deep into the reality of the role religion played in America in the eighteenth century. Religious and political freedoms were perceived as indivisibly linked.

At that time, religion was very much alive in American society. It has been estimated that between 1700 and 1776, sixty percent of the adult population attended church regularly. Popular sermons were printed by the thousands; up to the revolution in fact, devotional publications were by far the largest category of published material. (1)

No single denomination constituted a majority throughout the colonies. This fact helped create an atmosphere of religious tolerance. Whereas dissent concerned only an estimated seven percent in England, it was the daily reality for two thirds of the colonials. (2) Due to a lack of ordained priests, the local parishes operated under a higher degree of autonomy than was the case in Europe. They often elected lay elders to operate in the absence of mandated clergy. Thus, from the very beginning and for the most varied reasons, attendance had a voluntary character. The congregation felt it had a voice in its own affairs. The various denominations sidestepped many of the organizational obstacles by choosing leaders from the laity and forming congregations at will, thereby increasing their popular appeal.

Many churchgoers cared little for doctrine, often choosing affiliations according to proximity and convenience. Therefore there was fluidity between faiths. The issues influencing religious affiliation were often social rather than ideological. Churches provided much of the colonial education, assured assistance to the poor or created societies for women and youth. In this fluid situation two new streams developed from traditional religion. One would later be called evangelical, the other liberal.

The evangelical movement was the offspring of the Great Awakening, a religious stirring that swept over America and culminated in the years 1739 to 1745. Central to its message was the experience of conversion or salvation, which was characterized by a strong personal element. The evangelicals wanted to move towards a simpler creed of the heart; they also wanted to give full support to itinerant preaching. Compared with the traditional clergy, the evangelicals were either American-born or had emigrated early in life. The traditionalists were practically all educated abroad.

From another direction came the liberal movement, a reflection of the ideas of the enlightenment as they had developed in Europe, mainly by English and French philosophers such as Voltaire, Rousseau, Algernon Sidney and Locke. The ideas that mostly expressed themselves through political channels in Europe found easy acceptance within the American congregations. Whereas the evangelicals appealed to the new dogma of salvation, the liberals stripped religious creed of all but the bare essentials. What they professed was a Natural Religion. In practice, a new faith without dogma and trust in science went separate ways. Jonathan Mayhew, a Massachussets liberal minister, delivered sermons that were for the most part political in content. His 1750 sermon 'Discourse Concerning Unlimited Submission and Non Resistance to the Higher Powers' was later called the 'warning gun of American Revolution'. Likewise he was one of the first to oppose the Stamp Act with another political sermon.

When the shooting began, the religious dividing lines proved of no consequence in the matter of loyalties to revolution or crown. The revolution found a strong support among the clergy. The development of religious ideas reflected a conspicuous difference between the American experience and the socio-political conditions in Europe.

America had no feudal heritage and no strongly established church hierarchy. The situation in Europe had often brought about a strong polarization around religious matters: religious orthodoxy on one hand, anti-religious feelings on the other. That was particularly the case in France, and the major difference setting the stage for the American drama.

Benjamin Franklin: a Forerunner

Benjamin's Franklin's life encompasses practically the whole of the 18th century. Many of the tendencies living in the century find in Franklin a significant representative. Unlike most, if not all of his contemporaries, in Franklin the roads of science and religion never separated. Thus for him the term 'philosophy', equivalent to knowledge or science, stands for both natural and moral philosophy. In fact he asserts: "...there is no rank in natural knowledge of equal dignity and importance with that of being a good parent, a good child,... in short a good Christian". Chief among his concerns was the social realm.

Before age twenty-one, the young printer already left behind the rigorous Puritanism of Boston. In his autobiography he reveals that at age fifteen he started doubting Biblical revelation, and at age twenty-four he practically abandoned attendance to Sunday worship. Contrary to his contemporaries, his rejection of dogma did not lead him towards the purely rationalistic outlook of the liberals. He is only twenty-two when he wrote his Articles of Belief and Acts of Religion , including motives of adoration, petition and duty. It is in effect an equivalent of a personal daily worship. At age twenty-four, Franklin was projecting a 'United Party for Virtue' or more expressively ' The Society of the Free and Easy', by "forming the virtuous and good men of all nations into a regular body, to be governed by suitable good and wise rules."

In recapturing the philosopher's ideas we may come to define what Franklin calls the 'Art of Virtue', the book he never managed to write. Franklin's art of virtue is right action, " For doing the good to me is the only service in our power; and to imitate his beneficiences is to glorify Him."

Right action is subordinated to right thinking. " Evil as evil can never be chosen" he reminds us, "and though evil is often the effect of our own choice, yet we never desire it but under the appearance of ordinary good." Thus, although right thinking, the prerequisite to good action, sounds simple, in reality it isn't. Its main enemy is passion, which only allows us to appreciate the consequences of our actions in the immediate present, not those that follow. Reason lets us perceive the immediate and future effects of our deeds. However, reason alone isn't sufficient for it can be obscured by pride and ambition. Therefore, to be able to use reason as a tool of discernment, we must be able to conduct a dispassionate self-analysis.

At an early stage of his life, Franklin gave this self-analysis the form of the 'Thirteen Virtues' (temperance, order, silence, resolution....) These he classified according to a personal hierarchy of importance. According to this method, he practiced each virtue a week at a time. In a year, the whole set of virtues could be practiced exactly four times. Naively intended as a device for attaining perfection, the system became for Franklin a tool for self-awareness, showing him his weaknesses and promoting personal improvement. Through such an early accurate procedure, Franklin became a modern scientist in inner development, endeavoring to observe himself, much like he would later observe electricity. This personal way of testing himself and acknowledging his own errors and shortcomings led Franklin to an independent view of morality. He called it 'moral algebra', a way of weighing the pros and cons of his deeds and taking time before making important decisions. Franklin was thus breaking the ground for a new vision of morality, one no longer dictated by religion or external moral precepts but by individual consciousness.

Franklin's 'religion' was intimately personal and to quite a degree scientific, rather than just rational; it stemmed from some very new and unprecedented ideas, such as the ability to look at the inner life with scientific detachment. His central message of 'let conscience be your guide' would be taken on and refined by Emerson in the next century.

Chapter 2

From Saint Tammany to Washington's Day: Evolution of a Holiday

"We, Pennsylvanians these old tales reject,
And our own saint think proper to elect;
Immortal Tammany, of Indian Race!
Great in the Field, and foremost in the chace!
(Character of St Tammany, popular poem of 1786)

It may come as a surprise to start a review of American Festivals with a festival no longer celebrated, or even remembered. We do this, however, in order to shed light on some little known aspects of American history, and form a link with Washington's Day. The latter survives at present with the name of Presidents' Day, a celebration in homage of both Washington and Lincoln.

Imagine a May Day celebration in Colonial America. A maypole, decorated with flowers and ribbons, is erected in the middle of the square or other public location. The dancers, each holding a ribbon, move in a circle around the pole. A small band plays pennywhistles, drums and other instruments. Yet, upon closer examination we notice something odd. The participants are performing dances in a Native American style. In the midst of the performance the company is interrupted by the arrival of people dressed as Native Americans whooping and singing the war song. After completing their appearance, the newcomers collect money and retire satisfied. It is the custom for the participants on this day to wear a piece of buck-tail - symbol of liberty - in their hat or any other prominent part of their dress. The festivities are followed with the recitation of songs and poems in which a certain Tammany was remembered and exalted, often with a mix of solemnity and humoresque.

The scene described above is a May Day in honor of Saint Tammany as was celebrated in Annapolis, Maryland, in 1771. Other similar festivities were celebrated in many parts of the colonies in the years before, during and after the Revolution. (1)

Who was Tammany? It is in fact the Anglicization of the Algonquian Lenni Lenape name Tamanend. That a Tamanend existed we know from the 'Wallam Olum' or Red Score, a record of pictographs of the Lenni Lenape that covers Native American history from its origins up to the 17th century. (2) In fact three Tamanends were recorded in it. According to the estimates of Mc Cutchen, based on the Wallam Olum, the first Tamanend reigned some time during the 6th century A. D. Tamanend II was most likely a contemporary of the Iroquois League, and Mc Cutchen estimates that he probably lived around the year 1450. (3)

The name Tamanend means literally 'beaverlike'. It can be translated as *affable*, since the beaver was considered the most sociable of animals by the Lenape. Before the advent of the Iroquois League in the 1400-1500s, the Lenape formed one of the most powerful Native American leagues. Tamanend I and II acquired fame through their ability to bring peace; both concluded a peace with their enemies the Sioux. Tamanend II also assured peace with the Iroquois. Under their reigns, all the tribes could wander freely in their neighboring territories, hunt, fish and farm, provided that permission was sought. It was also possible to safely navigate the waterways. The perpetual threat of attacks and reprisals from traditional enemies was provisionally overcome under their reigns. Tamanend I, and most likely Tamanend II, besides being political rulers were also high priests of the Midewiwan - initiates of the Native American spiritual schools. For this reason they both were called the "First One'.

Tamanend III was the only ruler that the colonials could have known. His reign occurred at a time when the Lenni Lenape had lost their splendor and had begun to be subjugated by the Iroquois. His name rarely appears in any official document, although he gave rise to legends, such as the one indicating that he set himself on fire and died to save his honor. (4) Presumably he was the Sachem, leader of the Lenni Lenape, who brought about the Great Peace Treaty with William Penn, but no historical evidence bears proof of it. The peace resulting from the treaty lasted beyond Penn's death for at least thirty-six years.

Whether historical or not the similarity of Tamanend III with his predecessors is found in his ability to bring about a lasting peace. At the time of Tamanend III, the Moravian missionaries, such as Heckewelder, had already started to circulate the old Lenni Lenape legends and history. Thus it is more than likely that the Tammany of the colonials was a historical-mythical composite of the three Tamanend.

The 'amiable' Saint's career follows a circuitous path. The first mention of Tammany appears in 1732 in the records of the Schuylkill Fishing Company. It was a common custom to adopt a patron saint and the company had taken Tammany as their own. The revered patron and other Indian chiefs, according to their adopted traditions, granted the members of the society the right to fish and hunt within prescribed limits of woods and waters. The saint's celebration happened to be celebrated on May Day simply because that was the beginning of the fishing season. Thus a genius of fate contrived to bring about the association of ideas later adopted by patriotic societies.

Apparently, as we can learn from letters of the epoch, Tammany was celebrated in spontaneous fashion. The Tammany Societies at this point had a social and benevolent character. The popularity of Tammany in Pennsylvania was undeniable; as early as 1771, possibly earlier, he had found good company with the other saints celebrated throughout the year.

A modern remnant of the popularity of Tammany is to be found today in Philadelphia. At the eastern end of Market Street, overlooking the Delaware River at Penn's Landing, is a ten to twelve-foot high bronze statue of a Native American with long flowing hair, standing on top of a fifteen-foot pedestal. Over his shoulder is an eagle which holds the famous wampum-belt of the Great Peace Treaty signed by Penn with the Lenni Lenape in 1682. A caption indicates that this is Tamanend, the American patron saint, who was held in great esteem by the colonists and celebrated yearly on May 1st.

There is also a Celtic connection to the holiday. The Celts celebrated Beltane on May 1st, one of the four cardinal yearly celebrations and one of their major sacred days. In some parts of Germany the previous eve is 'Walpurgisnacht'. It was named after the daughter of king Richard the Lion Hearted, Saint Walpurga, a nun who had died a martyr. On that night witches were believed to fly, and that is how Walpurga came to be known as a protector against magic. Throughout the centuries May Day stood as a celebration of spring and the forces of renewal. In many places it was a day when social rules were turned upside down, a day for dancing and reveling. Early America had brought about a 'pagan saint'- a syncretistic celebration of Celtic and Native American inspiration. As we shall see, this amalgamation of Native American and Celtic traditions brings to light a very real but little known part of American history or prehistory.

Celtic and Native American Cultures: Evidence of Contact

After examining the historical record, there can be little doubt that the Bering Strait was not the only route for populating the Americas. What follows is a brief review of the evidence of a Celtic presence in America.

In ancient Irish manuscripts of the Middle Ages, reference was made to a land in the Far West called Iarghal, meaning "Beyond the Sunset". Pope Paschal II appointed Erik Gnupsson the first bishop of Greenland and Vinland (Norse name for the North Eastern shores of America) in the year 1112. This seems to show that contacts between the two sides of the Atlantic have been more frequent than later history reveals. (5)

Much of early American history lay dormant for centuries for lack of a way to decode it. All of this was due to an apparent enigma. There are recordings in Ireland of an alphabet called Ogam. The oldest reference to it appears in the Book of Leinster compiled by a bishop of Kildare, called Finn Mac Gorman, in 1160- A. D. Other similar books record many varieties of the Ogam alphabet. Ogam is a language using up to five simple short bars across a main line. It can be written from right to left or left to right, upwards or downwards. It was often also used as a rebus by slightly distorting the bars in order to approximate the represented object. It is an alphabet that was derived from finger language and in which the bars on either side of the main line replace the fingers. (6) Ogam was used by the so-called Goidelic or Q-Celts. These were the Celts of Ireland and Scotland as well as those of the

Iberian peninsula. The P-Celts of Brettany, Cornwall, Wales, and Gaul, used Greek or Latin letters.

Ogam has never been found in the British Isles, therefore the suspicion persisted that it was not a true language. No traces of it remain after the inscriptions were apparently erased throughout the following centuries of Christianity. This presented an apparent insoluble dilemma. While in Europe scholars could find no traces of Ogam writing, their American counterparts could not decipher endless amounts of American inscriptions. Traces of some varieties of Ogam do appear however in Spain and Portugal, and these are of the same kind found on American soil. Of all varieties of Ogam used in America the most common of them contained only consonants and is therefore called Ogam Consaine.

The inscriptions are not the only proof of a Celtic presence on the continent. The most telling evidence is the presence of megalithic monuments usually associated with the Old World. Such monuments include dolmens, megalithic stones and circles, and slab-roofed chambers. Their major concentration occurs in New England.

Standing megaliths, man-sized and higher, carrying Ogam inscriptions appear in Vermont, Connecticut, Massachusetts, New Hampshire, New Jersey, New York and Pennsylvania. Dolmens were megalithic tombstones covered with earth. They were generally dedicated to a chief or an event of importance. At the base lay a very large rock, generally flat, functioning as a table and balanced atop three rocks. That such dolmens could not be attributed to random effects of receding glaciers is evidenced by the fact that the supporting stones are set at multiples of the so-called megalithic yards, often in 3:4:5 relationships or golden ratio proportions, giving the shape of a right triangle. (7)

The most obvious similarity with Celtic monuments lies in the so-called 'root cellars', originally thought to have been built by colonists to protect their root crops. These 'root cellars' are rectangular or square buildings up to 30 feet long, 10 feet wide and 8 feet high (or higher). They were either completely buried, or partially, or completely exposed. The roof was made of slabs of long flagstone, weighing up to several tons. Colonists did not have the means or the need to go to such lengths merely to preserve roots. Furthermore, the method would have been very ineffective. But what is most telling is the additional fact that, like their European counterparts, everything in the way they were built shows that they were used for similar astronomical purposes. They nearly always face 23.5 degrees East, the direction of the Winter Solstice sunrise observation. The outer surface of the door lintel often carries Ogam dedications to a Celtic God, usually Bel, the Sun God. At the western end a smoke hole is located above the altar, indicating the use of altar fire. Other open-air observatories make use of platforms surrounded in a circle by megaliths which indicate the positions of the sunrise for both solstices and equinoxes. [8] Finally, stone rings, single or double, of up to ten feet in diameter or more, have also been found throughout New England primarily, but also elsewhere as far west as Nevada and California. [9] At Mystery Hill, New Hampshire, a site open to the public, a large number of such slab-roofed chambers and megaliths are clustered.

Communications between both sides of the Atlantic seem to have varied according to the degree of ease offered by the glaciations. At the peak of the Bronze Age, which started at around 2000 B. C., the polar ice melted. Communication with America was then much easier. After 1200 B. C., the world climate cooled off again, and did so until 700 A. D. The first eloquent proof of Northern European presence in America is to be found at the time of the Bronze Age, roughly at around 1700 B. C. This was documented by Barry Fell in the book Bronze Age America, in which he presents the results of his efforts to decode the inscriptions of the site known as Petroglyph Park at Peterborough, near Toronto, Canada. Here the inscriptions are written in Tifinag, an earlier form of alphabet preceding the Ogam. This alphabet used symbols to identify letters. Thus the letter *s* comes from *sun* symbolized by concentric circles. In Barry Fell's words, it is as if "the ancient Nordic people looked at the sky and saw the letters written large upon the face of the heaven". Evidence of Tifinag is present everywhere in Scandinavia. In Peterborough, Fell has brought forth evidence of the establishment of a trading colony established by a Nordic king, Woden-Lithi, who sailed across the Atlantic to Canada via the St. Lawrence River. His homeland was in Norway at Ringerike, west of the head of the Oslo Fjord. He remained in Canada for a time, trading woven material for copper, seventeen centuries before our era. [10]

Much of the evidence represented in Peterborough shows the pictographic images of the Norse and Celtic gods. Sunu, the Norse equivalent of Bel, appears there as the solar ship carrying the sun across the heavens by day and beneath the earth by night. All the other gods appear likewise. These include Woden, Thor, Loki, Tsiw, the son of Odin, and others. Many mythological accounts of the deeds of the Aesir (sky gods), Wanir (earth gods), as well as of their enemies, the giants and monsters, are represented in various pictographs. This northern influx of people is different from the Western Celtic and pre-Celtic immigrants that we will talk about, and the mythology here referred to is particular to Scandinavian and Germanic people. These two population groups share paths, as we can see from other evidence throughout northern America. At that historical moment, as the work of Barry Fell shows, there still was little linguistic differentiation between the populations of Northern Europe, from Scandinavia to the Baltic shores, Germany and Britain.

This isn't the place to fully prove the presence of Nordic, pre-Celtic and later Celtic immigrants to the New World. Others have done it exhaustively. However, readers may find it of value if we briefly enumerate some elements of the fascinating evidence.

Many kinds of tools found in America match almost perfectly the equivalent tools extracted from British barrows. These include stone axe heads, bone arrow heads and lance heads To this list we can add all the objects found at Andover, Massachusetts: javelin points, axe-heads, hammer-stones, drills, mauls, pestles, polished celts, all of them similar to objects found in Europe. (11) The presence of bronze weapons similar to the Celtic equivalents in Mound Builder sites (an otherwise rare occurrence), remains a puzzle because the tin necessary for the alloy is not found in North America. (12)

Other relevant confirmation of Celtic presence comes from the American West. Petroglyphs from British Columbia, Alberta and Nevada, indicating the presence of both Norse and Celts in the West, illustrate the various stages of sheep farming and transformation of the wool. The petroglyphs are accompanied by Ogam Celtic or Norse inscriptions. In one of these petroglyphs, plowing with oxen is represented. This suggests a memory of an Old World farming practice. (13)

Mc Clone and Leonard have found Celtic vestiges in Colorado, attested by the presence of Ogam inscriptions in Gaelic. (14)

A distinction should be made between the megalithic monuments and the accompanying inscriptions. Scholars generally agree that the megaliths go back to the Neolithic times; they are the work of populations that predated the Celts, although there was an uninterrupted cultural continuity between these and the later Celts. Ogam writing is a much more recent invention, dating from a time shortly before or after the beginning of our era *(most likely 200 A. D.)*. Although the American monuments have not yet been properly dated, the evidence may reveal a Celtic and pre-Celtic presence in the continent much earlier than previously thought. On the basis of radiocarbon dating, Barry Fell gives 850 B. C. as the earliest date.

Native Americans have maintained faithful representations of the Celtic and Norse gods, accompanied by the corresponding Ogam inscriptions, even when the alphabets were no longer used. Such are the petroglyphs of the Takhelne tribe in British Columbia. Along the Milk River of South Alberta are representations of Woden and his steed Sleipnir, or Thor. The representations date from the last two-three centuries, since they are carved in a nonresistant rock. This attests to the remarkable faculties of mnemonic preservation of the Native Americans. (15) Evidence of the observation of the festival of Beltane itself at Mystery Hill (N. H.), shows that it fell on the 39th day of the Roman calendar (39 days after the spring equinox). This illustrates the complete accord that existed between the dates of the Celtic festivals in Europe and the equivalent festivals in America. (16)

The joint evolution of Native American and Celtic spirituality may have left more traces than previously believed. The civilization of Cahokia, the famous Mound-builders of the Mississippi area, flourished between 700 and 1300 A. D. In this old metropolis we find the vestiges of what has been dubbed 'Woodhenge'. Near the highest mound, Monk's Mound, archaeologists have found the wooden foundations of four large circles with diameters varying between 240 and 480 feet. Each circle was made of 48 posts evenly spaced. The posts averaged 2' in diameter. The whole structure is believed to be a sun calendar used for the observation of solstices and equinoxes. (17)

No less interesting are the oldest and best preserved Medicine Wheels: Big Horn Medicine Wheel in Wyoming, and Moose Mountain Medicine Wheel in Saskatchewan. They are both built with rocks and boulders, forming a wheel with spokes. The Big Horn wheel measures 25 feet in diameter and has a central hub with 28 spokes. Their dates of construction are estimated at 650 to 1050 A. D. for Moose Mountain and 1050-1450 for Big Horn. Some of the spokes marked with cairns on the circle point towards the rising and setting points of conspicuous stars: Aldebaran, Rigel and Sirius according to the researchers Robinson and Fries. [(18)]

It is curious to see how the above structures were replicated for a completely different use in the much later ritual of the sun dance. This ceremony uses a wooden lodge built over a circle with 28 posts at the periphery supporting the poles that stretch from the periphery towards a higher post placed at the center. [(19)] All the above puzzling monuments or structures seem to be the result of Celtic and Native American cultural interplay. The old elements of Celtic culture appear either modified or serving a new purpose.

In light of all the evidence of contact between the two cultures of the West presented above, it becomes less surprising that a Celtic tradition with Native American overtones was popular during Colonial times.

From King to Saint, from Tammany to Washington

Tammany had a later career after the one already described. He became in effect a political figure. The patriotic character of the 'friendly Saint' was probably born around the year 1765, when colonial resistance to the British Crown surged, after the passing of the Stamp Act. In the press his name was 'King Tammany'. In 1772 the first permanent society in Philadelphia was named the "Sons of King Tammany", a name echoing the "Sons of Liberty". Later in that year the press started mentioning the native leader as either king or saint.

At this time Tamanend's career rapidly accelerated. At the outbreak of the Revolution, the Pennsylvania troops adopted the saint as patron and guide. Shortly after the Continental Army followed suit. By now May Day was observed both at home and on the field, and had clearly taken on a larger dimension than the borders of Pennsylvania. It was in the same year that John Leacock wrote a successful patriotic play with a very long title: " The Fall of the British Tyranny or American Liberty Triumphant...." An ode in this comedy, written in honor of Saint Tammany in a rather burlesque tone, became popular and was later sung at the celebrations of the Tammany Societies. Tammany's effigy even found its way into the national flag on May Day 1785, in Philadelphia. [20]

The above are some of the recorded landmarks of Tammany's odyssey from historical figure to quasi-national symbol. Patron saints were a familiar occurrence among all kinds of societies in the 18th century. Nations themselves adopted saints. In the years before the Revolution, many foreign societies had adopted their national saints. These were all loyal to the crown. Choosing a native saint was a way of establishing a distance from tradition and setting oneself apart from all other loyalist societies. It was also a way to cover–up revolutionary activities with what had hitherto been benevolent and social charities. Nevertheless, the symbolic status of Tamanend was never an intentional design. It seems rather to have followed a natural progression from jest to eventual defiance.

The Saint's popularity did not abate after independence was achieved. Stories and songs flourished from 1773 to 1789. A 'myth' that gained considerable popularity was even written in 1795 by Samuel Latham Mitchill, professor at Columbia College, scientist and politician. His is a myth of the overcoming of seven stages of evil by a certain Tammany, initiate and civilizing hero. [21] In this modern myth Tammany has to face seven tests. The first three ordeals involve natural catastrophes. Tammany overcomes them through the use of natural remedies. The fourth attack comes in the form of a war declared by the neighboring tribes. Tammany vanquishes the attackers. Afterwards, showing clemency, he reconciles them with unexpected generosity and brings about a lasting peace. After this stage, in what is the turning point of the myth, the evil one decides to treacherously attack Tammany. Following a fifty-day battle Tammany subjugates the foe, without totally vanquishing him. Makimanito - as the enemy is called - is relegated to the far north. Tammany then dedicates himself to the arts of peace, such as the introduction of new agricultural practices and technical innovations. In the absence of Tammany, Makimanito attacks the tribes' moral fiber. Idleness and depravity give rise to illness and disease. Tammany can heal them through his knowledge of the properties of medicinal herbs.

The saint's popularity spread as far south as Louisiana, and as far north as New York. Further north Tammany would have made odd company with puritan traditions. Pilgrims took a dim view of wild celebrations. This attitude was probably reinforced after the Pilgrim's uproar over the May Day revels at Merry Mount (near Plymouth Rock), a joint Indian and colonial celebration featuring ample use of alcohol. Still, it is very likely that the Sons of Liberty were in contact with the various Tammany Societies, and such a link has been established for the Saint Tamina (sic.) Society of Annapolis, Maryland. That the Sons of Liberty also adopted some of the Native American values and disguises is widely known. The famous Boston Tea Party of 1773 was performed by forty or fifty patriots dressed as Mohawks. Finally, while the New Englanders didn't dance around the maypole, they assembled more soberly around the Liberty Tree.

The Saint Tammany societies were later revived in the Orders of Red Men and the Improved Orders of Red Men. This was a way to circumvent a decree by the Secretary of War, issued in 1812, forbidding the practices of the Tammany Societies in the army and qualifying them as debauching to the troops. The Societies of Red Men preserved the observance of Saint Tammany's Day but moved it to May 12th. They were instituted for social and mutual assistance purposes, as well as for charity, and committed to the defense of the Constitution. Their motto was "freedom, friendship and charity." Their ritual had all the ethos of a Freemason society. [22]

The reviving of the Tammany ideal in conjunction with Masonry and the canonization of Tammany the king point back to a time when the process of initiation was still possible and was practiced within the sacred centers. Tamanend is both a spiritual and a political leader; we may say he is a political leader precisely because first and foremost he is a spiritual leader. It is in his status as an initiate of the

Midewiwin that he can infuse spiritual values into his culture, and therefore bring the blessings of peace. The choice of May Day - said to be a day of openness between the physical world and the spiritual world - reinforces this meaning.

At the time of the colonies, this medieval view of the enlightened king was coming to an end, not only in Europe, but also in Northern America. It was going to be supplanted by the Iroquois model, as we will see in Chapter 3. In the earlier times of the Colonies, especially on the East Coast of present day United States, many confederacies, ruled by the equivalent of a king, still existed. We will see two of them in Chapter 5: the Powhatan confederacy in Virginia and the Wampanoag confederacy in Massachussets. Tamanend stands both as a beginning and an end - a beginning in the way he inspires ideals for the Revolution - an end in as much as the monarchy gradually gives way to new, more complex forms of government.

The Tammany Societies all across the colonies named Washington as their Grand Sachem. Before becoming the country's first president, Washington had accumulated many other honorific titles. He was the president of the Cincinnatus Society, an organization founded by Army officers and committed to a strong Union. The Pennsylvania Grand Lodge, in 1779, had harbored the idea of a nationwide Grand Lodge with Washington as its president, and Virginia chose him as the Grand Lodge Master in 1778, but he declined.

Washington's birthday was honored with festivities for the first time in 1782, on the occasion of his fiftieth birthday in Richmond, Virginia. It was celebrated the following year with a banquet in New York, and repeated in 1784 after the withdrawal of the English troops. Until that time it had not become a recurring celebration. That came about with the inauguration of Washington's first term as president. This celebration came in great part through the initiative of the Tammany Societies, especially in New York. For that reason, some did in fact call it the Tammany Observance. Washington's name was associated in jest with his illustrious predecessor, as it appears from the lines of the Ode for Saint Tammany's Day:

"Now each Sachem join hands round the Liberty Pole,
And briskly again pass the heart cheering bowl;
To Washington's mem'ry, the chief of our train,
The full flowing goblet repeated we'll drain...."
(from Ode for St Tammany's Day, May 1st 1785) (23)

Washington was thus elevated to the image of the 'affable saint', and to the status of a 'First One'. That the patron saint received a human counterpart was not any great departure from tradition. The British crown and other monarchies honored both king and saint; Saint George had his day, as much as the king had his own. This tradition hearkened back to the king as the agent of divine will on earth. However, in the very first year in which his birthday was celebrated, Washington refused the crown that the Colonel Lewis Nicola offered him in the name of the Army. Perhaps he realized that an era had come to an end. We can appreciate what stood behind the figure of Washington with a view at the most characteristic elements of his life.

Recurring Themes in George Washington's Life

This brief biography of Washington will also serve as an introduction to the following chapter. Washington's life marks a transition and we will show how he brings a certain ideal to a culmination and end - precisely what can be called 'the Tammany ideal'. On the other hand he inaugurates a new epoch, as we will see in the following chapter.

Understanding a national figure requires the basic understanding of national and international phenomena. Central to coming to terms with this individual is a bare-bones knowledge of what some have called 'mercantilism', the unstated economic doctrine of British imperialism. Therefore, in order to better understand Washington and the times in which he lived, we turn to the economic sphere of life at the time of the Colonies.

The reasons that led to the American Revolution are often enumerated in the Stamp Act, Townsend Acts and the Navigation Acts, suggesting that these marked a sudden change in the nature of the relationship between mother country and colonies. These acts were in fact only the catalysts of a rebellion, but the logical outcome of the kind of economic relationships that had ruled ever since the beginning of the colonies.

After the Middle Ages, the economic growth of nations would have been unconceivable without the growth of military power to sustain it. Wealth was conceived in terms of gold and silver, and economic advantage derived from a favorable balance of trade. England expected exactly that from America, as from any other colony. Thus, as early as 1660, economic activity and growth were everywhere regulated or curtailed in American soil by the Council of Trade - later called the Board of Trade. No export could leave America for a third country without first reaching England. Imports other than of English origin were submitted to duties. In practice trade was in the hands of what could be called virtual monopolies, and the middlemen would realize large profits at the expense of the colonists. The trade surplus generated by England went to pay the Crown's internal debt. From the combined efforts of the English policies it has been estimated that the balance of trade between the Colonies and England, between the years 1700 and 1773, was of 30,000,000 pounds in favor of England. Part of that amount served to pay the debt of the Crown. This debt amounted to 74,000,000 pounds in 1775; the interest on this sum was of 2,400,000.[(24)] In the years just before the Revolution, England realized a profit of 3,000,000 pounds per year from American trade.

Among the consequences brought forth by the rules of the Board of Trade was the repeated prohibition of manufacturing activities [(25)], prohibition of exports, and finally the curtailing of the growth of the territories due to the difficulty of enforcing the law over an ever-growing expanse of land. The reaction to rampant smuggling brought about the recourse to searches without warrant and trials without jury.

It was in the South that British mercantilism found its ultimate logical outcome in the system of plantations operated by slaves. Ever since the introduction of tobacco codified monopolistic practices were enforced. In 1619 the Crown was imposing duties on colonial tobacco. Two years later it prohibited the sale of tobacco to any other country without first landing in England and paying the duty. The following year the Virginia Company was awarded monopoly of importation in England and Ireland. When the planters started to sell tobacco to other colonies, especially New England, a prohibitive duty eliminated that possibility. The net result of these policies was to drastically reduce the price of tobacco, while the price of imported goods was beyond the colonists' control. This ushered in the extensive use of slaves, over which the British had acquired the monopoly following the wars with the Dutch. Before the Navigation Acts, the Southern colonies could sell their tobacco to the Dutch for three pence per pound. By 1767, after the Navigation Acts, tobacco prices had fallen to a half penny per pound. The same Navigation Acts raised the prices of imports, now confined to British ships. More competitive sources, like the Dutch, had been precluded. Slavery became a recourse for the planters in order to cut production costs. English laws prevented the South from restricting the slave trade. For equivalent reasons New England and the Middle Colonies later became major actors in the slave trade. [(26)]

Mercantilism can thus be defined as the complete identification of economic and political interests. Where economic competition was barred from exerting its benefits, it could only be supported with the complicity of the political system. A prominent political class and often the Crown itself benefited in England from the formation of immense economic monopolies. While on one hand English tradition advocated the liberties of the Englishman, on the other hand economic monopolies were promoted at the expense of these very same liberties. America was unique among the colonies in the fact that here mercantilism was imposed not upon a native population, but for the most part among subjects of His Majesty, well acquainted with the tradition of individual liberties.

It is significant that from the indebted and economically shackled South came George Washington, a Virginia native. Virginia also gave the nation the considerable contributions of Mason, Madison, Jefferson, Randolph, Patrick Henry and numerous others.

Washington had unusually striking and prominent physical features and an imposing stature. He had very large hands, joints and feet, and long arms and legs. His hips were broad, his neck has been described as 'superb' by George Mercer. He also had a large mouth. He was truly 'head and shoulders above the rest'.

As might be imagined, he possessed a robust physical constitution. As a youth he had a taste for physical prowess. He was an excellent horse rider and renowned dancer. His life was filled with brushes with death or illness. He survived malaria at seventeen, smallpox two years later, dysentery at age twenty-five. In 1789 he had a tumor removed from his thigh and the following year came close to dying from a combination of influenza and pneumonia. Another example will illustrate his physical strength. At age twenty-one Washington was attempting to cross the partly frozen Allegheny in a raft. The raft became stuck in the ice and Washington fell overboard. He had to spend a chilling night on an island until he could cross over the frozen river the next day. Amazingly, he survived without consequences. In contrast, his companion Christopher Gist had all his fingers and some toes frozen. Even more famous is an episode during the French and Indian war. In an assault on a hill, Washington, ill at the time, had two horses shot from underneath him, and managed to find a third one. During the battle a bullet hit his hat, three other ones his uniform.

There was in Washington's character a trait of steadfastness, oscillating between the extremes of ambition and impulsiveness, and a continuous desire for self-improvement. An episode, which purportedly occurred during his days as a burgess for the Virginia Assembly, is a case in point. During a political campaign Washington apparently offended a fellow by the name of Payne, who in turn hit him with a hickory branch. Washington appeared the next day, not to pursue the matter further but to offer his apologies. It is well-known that as a boy he copied down pages from Francis Hawkins' Youth's Behavior. Later he would replace this first model with the play Cato by Addison - his favorite reading.

At age twenty-one Washington joined the Fredericksburg Masonic Lodge. Masonry provided a continuing thread in Washington's life and much of his outlook can be understood in light of it. Masonry was not an abstract philosophy, for which he had little inclination, but a code of honor that could pervade and accompany all his actions. Masonic loyalties molded the relationships within the Army and a Masonic inauguration brought him to the presidency. Of this more will be said later.

Washington also had a regular and deep life of prayer. He ordered prayers to be said in the Army every morning and on Sunday. When no chaplain was available he would say the prayers himself. We can detect in him deep mystical leanings.

For all his ambition, pride and impulsive nature, Washington displayed quite other qualities as well. He was a reticent and careful speaker and a good listener. He was also sensitive to what others thought of him. Washington was to remain thin-skinned practically to the end. Such was his striving for integrity and a higher code of conduct that he could not understand how his intentions could be misconstrued. Foregoing popular support was one of Washington' s repeated major tests.

Washington's need to release his over-abundant will in order to devote it for a higher purpose finds a fitting symbol in the odd way in which he cared for his teeth. It is hard to imagine what would induce a man to lose practically all his teeth from cracking walnuts between his jaws, endure the pain of the ensuing inflammations, and the irritation of a denture carved from hippopotamus tusks. Yet this was precisely Washington's practice.

Turning points in Washington's biography's coincide with major events in American history. At age twenty-one he volunteered on a diplomatic mission to the French, shortly before what became the French and Indian War. Soon after, he started his military career in the very same conflict. Exactly twenty-one years later this constellation of events recurred on a higher level. It was again a turning point between diplomatic efforts and a call for action, this time between British and Colonials. He was chosen as a Virginia delegate to the First Continental Congress, and a year later named Commander in Chief of the Continental Army.

The first forty-two years of Washington's life formed a stage of apprenticeship. During this period he had the opportunity to temper his ambition and impulsiveness with the obstacles put in the way by the colonial reality of the times. In more ways than one Washington was a quintessential representative of the grievances of his compatriots. As a planter he was deeply indebted and had to devise continuous ways towards self-sufficiency and independence, because the system of mono-culture made the plantation system a captive market of the English monopolies. His military career met with success as well as setbacks. He was promoted to colonel at Fort Necessity only to be demoted to the rank of captain later, an offer that he turned down. After becoming an aide-de-camp for Colonel Braddock he was named Commander in Chief but had to take second place to Dagworthy, a captain, since the latter was appointed by Royal Commission and Washington was only a Colonial. On the political front he had keenly felt how little power was vested in the Virginia House of Burgesses, twice dissolved during his tenure, when it tried to promote colonial economic independence. Washington reached the conclusion of the inevitable break with Britain. His conclusion was based, not on the ground of the ideals of Jefferson or Madison, but on the inner knowledge deriving from experience, leading him to take what he perceived as the right action. His decision was personal as much as political. The one and the other were completely linked in him. It was the realization of the South's economic state of dependence that led him to embrace the non-importation agreements in response to the Stamp Act. He went further on the personal level by turning away from tobacco and developing small processing industries on his lands. By this time he had paid-off his debt to Cary and Co., his suppliers.

From his experience of forty-two years Washington gained the knowledge of how to use his tempered will. This enabled him to take on the task of leading the Continental Army. During the war he had to constantly relinquish personal power in favor of the possibility of a new social experiment. Later on, after the victory of the Revolution, Washington vigorously exerted his power in order to defend the precarious new government against the dangers that threatened it from the outside – in particular the political threat of the French Revolution and the economic threat of the British.

During the war Washington had to coordinate his activities with Congress. He had fully understood the importance of a transparent, if not harmonious, cooperation with the political body. Soldiers, politicians and civilians had to be won over to the ideals of the Declaration of Independence, not once, but over and over again. Thus Washington endured all delays, divisions, and hesitations on the part of Congress. Likewise he did not retaliate personally against insubordination or political scheming within the Army. However, when the need arose he stood up against the Conway cabal. When absolute power was within reach he refused the crown offered to him by the Army, through Colonel Lewis Nicola in 1782. The following year he used all his personal influence to quell army mutinies and insurgency against Congress.

That the Constitutional Convention owes much to his presence is beyond doubt. His was a silent presence, though no less powerful for that fact. His stature and integrity contributed in large measure to the success of the Convention.

As we have mentioned, two significant sets of events stand out in Washington's presidency. One was the test posed by the French Revolution, the other the continuing English imperialism. Agents of the French Revolution were actively proselytizing around the world. In America the Revolution's envoy was 'Citoyen' Genet. Washington had initially reacted favorably to the political change. With time, the flaring of passions, the report of atrocities and the death toll of the guillotine made a different impression on the President. In 1793 war broke out between France and England, and Washington opted for a course of strict neutrality. It was a first trial of standing against popular opinion, and it prevented the young country from being engulfed in the French revolutionary zeal. On the English front, the president concluded a very unpopular treaty with England in 1795. Although more favorable to England, it was probably the most the United States could hope for, considering its obvious state of economic and military inferiority. At any rate, it allowed the nation to turn away from the European turmoil and build its own strength while avoiding war.

In Jefferson and Hamilton - at the State and Treasury Departments respectively - America's situation on the international front found a reflection within the Administration. They were in every aspect polar opposites. Jefferson was a man of passionate ideas - at moments naïve but always sincere. Hamilton had high intellectual capacities. He was a stern realist and a very ambitious one. His love for the new country was for the most part a love of its government. The difference between the two men is reflected in the nature of departments the two antagonists headed.

That Hamilton was a strong supporter of England needs no additional proofs. (27) He would have modeled the new nation in many degrees according to the old one. He was also in favor of a strong centralism, and often opted for displays of force before negotiation. However, he was probably one of the few who had the capacity to lead the nation to financial independence. In contrast Jefferson was a very strong supporter of State's rights and had been won over in a very determined way to the ideas of the French Revolution. (28) He later regretted his youthful ardor, at least in regard to his support of the French Revolution.

France's policy was a sort of 'all or nothing' attempt: trying to win national sympathy and support. For that it must be said that the ideas of the French Revolution would truly enflame people's minds in a rapturous passion, much as they did Jefferson's. England on the other hand could gain support for its plans by the appropriate politician in the right place, much as it tried through Hamilton. English agencies were disguised in the tools of trade and finance.

Washington held the ground between oligarchy and a pure democracy represented respectively by Hamilton and Jefferson. America became a republican government, as distinguished from a pure and simple popular democracy. The president knew how to use the two men's strength for the goals that the nation needed to achieve: foreign recognition and financial-economic independence.

Everything that has been said so far suggests strongly that Washington was the end-product of an epoch. He truly was the equivalent of a Tammany, a 'First One'. Jefferson and Hamilton, imperfect as they appear, are the necessary protagonists upon which the fabric of society would be built after Washington. New social compacts needed to materialize in the emerging nation. Other forces would had to supersede the last echoes of Native American and Celtic spirituality, represented in a syncretistic way by Saint Tammany. These we will discover in the Fourth of July chapter.

Chapter 3

Fourth of July: the Temple, the Lodge and the Longhouse

"Thy word is good, but a word is nothing until it is given form and sent to work in the world. What form shall the message take when it comes to dwell among men?"

(The White Roots of Peace, Paul A. W. Wallace)

No other public festival occupies such a central place in the United States as the Fourth of July. The inner essence of the occasion is recaptured in the famous words of the Declaration of Independence. "All men are created equal,…, they are endowed by their Creator with certain inalienable rights…".

The Declaration of Independence was the culmination of a long process whose roots extend into European and American territory. We turn our gaze to the three-four centuries before the Declaration – a period in which powerful forces of renewal were at work just beneath the surface of history. From there we pick-up the strands that worked independently in the British Islands and in North America. They converged and slowly wove into a tapestry that gave birth to the new federal form of government. We recognize three forces working with particular zeal to bring about a new reality in the social order before arriving at the Declaration of Independence. The first one of these is the order of the Knights Templar.

Knights Templar in America? The Zeno-Sinclair Expedition

We will take our starting point with a fascinating and little known expedition to colonize the New World by the most famous knights in history. The Zeno-Sinclair is the only documented expedition to the New World before Columbus. Its authenticity has been contested. We will gather abundant evidence of its occurrence. Why were the Templar knights – or rather their immediate successors – interested in the New World? What were their aims? We cannot answer these questions without looking at their history. To do so we limit our gaze to France, where the knights saw their official origin.

The Templars and the Transformation of the Social World

The order of the Knights Templar was started by Hugues de Payens in 1118, twenty years after the conquest of Jerusalem by the First Crusade. Payens is a small village close to Troyes, to the East of Paris. Hugues de Payens was in contact with the circles out of which emerged Chretien de Troyes' Le Conte du Graal, fifty years after the foundation of the order.

The Council of Troyes was called in 1128 at the time of the return of the first Knights Templar from Jerusalem. Its sole aim was the establishment of the rules of the new order. The Council delegated Bernard of Clairvaux, founder of the Cistercians, to write the rules. It seems that from its inception the Templars were meant to be the worldly arm of the Cistercians. Bernard wanted the order to generate riches, yet in such a way that they could only be used selflessly. Its members could not benefit from the wealth since they had taken a vow of poverty. The vow was extreme; no ransom would be paid for a captive Templar. This separation of roles between the orders of Cistercians and Templars is made evident by provisions such as Bernard's rule that the Cistercians receive no estate goods. These are reserved for the Templars. [(1)] The knights fought in the East, and in the West they offered their services and resources to the building of cathedrals. For the cathedrals to arise in their majesty, the Templars had to bring about a monumental feat – namely a complete transformation of the social order.

The basic structure of the Templar order was the 'commanderie'. It generally centered around a large farm, which served as headquarters for the Brethren. It hosted a church and was used for many social functions. A look at the Templar presence in France will show the extent to which the order penetrated the social fabric. In the 12th century there were an estimated 2000 commanderies, covering an equivalent of five million acres of land, and many more possessions in real estate. They owned approximately fifty houses in Troyes, their place of origin, and whole neighborhoods in Paris. Gradually, the commanderies spread like a grid over the whole of France and other countries of Europe. As a result, the Templars maintained a continual presence on the roads. They guaranteed the safety of travelers from criminals and also freed trade from the arbitrary tolls of innumerable civil authorities. The commanderies served as relay points along the roads, acted as hostels for the travelers, and even as repositories for temporary storage of goods.

In the process of developing trade, the Templars had quite naturally taken on the role of bankers. They were able to administer uniform practices. The people trusted them due to their solid reputation for integrity. The monastic rule of the order denied personal use of the riches generated by trade. Consequently, the continuously reinvested wealth further developed trade and accumulation of capital. It was this surplus of economic activity that enabled labor and resources to come together and accomplish the feat of building the great cathedrals. None of the cities of the time could have spared time and resources for this monumental undertaking. While the cathedrals are certainly the spiritual product of Citeaux, and what has been called the School of Chartres, their material manifestation is the product of the transformation of the social order brought about by the Templars.

History records that Philip the Fair, King of France, was drawn to the riches of the Templars. Quite aside from the element of greed, Philip saw in the Templars a social force at odds with his designs. From the beginning the Templars had received special privileges. They did not have to respond to any religious or political power, nor did they pay taxes. They could mint their own coin and owned large amounts of land and real estate. Entire villages were under their jurisdiction. In many ways they were a state within the State and a church within the Church. Philip perceived that the transformation of society brought about by the Templars was a threat to his own designs for power. The knights were setting precedents of autonomy from Church and State. In places, where they had legislation over small villages, they were setting the basis of a new social order by freeing the serfs. The king at the head of a very centralized state could hardly tolerate the spirit of reform emanating from the order. It comes as no surprise that Philip acted to arrest the Templars in 1307. In 1312 he obtained from the Pope a decree banning them.

In attempting to put an end to the power of the Templars, Philip the Fair faced a monumental task. It would have been almost impossible for him to muster the resources, soldiers and effect of surprise for mounting such an enterprise as the arrest of all the Templars and the seizure of all their possessions. Consequently, only a portion of the order was ever arrested and much of their famed treasure was never found. The reaction of all the kingdoms to the papal decree varied in intensity and degree. The persecution of the Templars was strongest in France. In Spain the Templars merged with other military orders that operated against the Moors: Calatrava and Montesa in particular. In Portugal the order continued to operate in a new form. Evidence shows that Portugal received the fugitive Templars and their fleet in the harbor of Serra del Rey. In 1320 the Portuguese king transformed the Templars into the Order of Christ. [(2)]

Although physically preserved in the Iberian peninsula, the Templars could not continue and evolve their mission in that region. They were losing their autonomy from either church or state. Only one land offered them that opportunity. This was Scotland, or rather the future Scotland.

The Sinclairs and the Rebirth of Scotland

To understand the role played by the Templars in Scotland, we shall have to look first at the extraordinary set of circumstances which led to their arrival in that land. Indispensable to these events was the Sinclair family, originally St. Clair. Like pieces added to a puzzle, we shall eventually see emerge the causes behind a little-known early colonization of America.

The St. Clair family finds its origin in the Viking occupation of Normandy in 911 A. D. At that time the family carried the name Møre. It was a family that controlled some of coastal Norway, the Orkney Islands and Caithness in Scotland. The founder of the family had been Earl Rongwald. One of his sons, Rolf, known as Rollo to the French, conquered Brittany and Normandy. In the year 911 he signed the

Treaty of St. Clair on the Epte River, in Normandy, with King Charles the Simple. After converting to Christianity, Rolf married the king's daughter and named himself the first Duke of Normandy. The name St. Clair derives from the name given to a Scottish saint of the 7th century, originally called Guillermus or William. He lived near a well whose waters were said to cure diseases of the eye, hence the name St. Clair. The name St. Clair or Sanctus Clarus originally meant *Holy Light.* (3)

The St. Clairs appear intimately associated with early Scottish history in more than one way. A William St Clair, called 'the Seemly' was the one who accompanied Margaret, the daughter of the English king Edmund Ironsides, in exile to Hungary during a time of succession struggles. From there Margaret took with her to Scotland what would later be called the Black Rood - a relic of the *true cross* enshrined in a gold and silver reliquary. Bringing the relic to Scotland was equal to confirming the divine right of the Scottish monarchy. William St. Clair became the keeper of the holy relic. His family was given as their blazon the 'engrailed' cross on their shields. Another anecdotal addition to the destiny of William the Seemly was also given by Margaret. Near Roslin, south of Edinburgh, is found a well emitting a mix of bitumen and oil that healed ailments of the skin. It was said to have been opened by Margaret upon releasing St. Katherine's blood brought from the tomb on Mount Sinai. William was given the lands of Roslin. The 7th Lord of Roslin was later made Guardian of the Crown Prince and the Blood Royal, which became a hereditary title. (4) As we will see, Roslin would later play an important role in the future development of the Templars in Scotland.

From a very early time the Scottish St. Clair were associated with the Templars. Hugh de Payens had married a French Catherine de St. Clair and set up the Templar headquarters at Balantrodoch, on St. Clair land, situated between two St. Clair castles. Members of the St. Clair family would later serve as canons of the Cistercians who were, as we have seen, closely associated with the Templars. (5)

Finally, the St. Clairs played an important role in the rebirth of the Scottish monarchy in the 1300. It is believed that the St. Clairs had links with the Bruce family from both the Orkneys and Normandy. The Bruces may originate from Brix, originally Brus in Normandy.

However, the evidence in this direction is not conclusive. Nonetheless, it is a fact that three St. Clairs fought alongside Robert de Bruce at Bannockburn on June 24, 1314 - St John's day - only three months after the death of Jacques de Molay at the stake. Bannockburn was the decisive turning point of Scottish independence from England.

From the above we can begin to see more clearly the elements that allowed for the survival of the Templar tradition in Scotland. The destiny of the Bruce family played a pivotal role. In 1292 Robert de Bruce had become Earl of Carrick, one of the most powerful fiefdoms of Scotland. In 1305, in the struggle for the Scottish succession, de Bruce murdered John Comyn, his rival, who had submitted to England. What gave this murder a special stamp was the fact that it was carried out inside a church, an affront to the authority of the Pope. As a result, Robert de Bruce was excommunicated in 1306.

Having lost the support of the Pope and needing forces to overthrow the English, it was natural for Robert de Bruce to turn to the Templars, whom the Pope had banned. However, he could not do this openly for fear of alienating his French allies. There is indirect evidence pointing to Ireland as the way of entry for the Templars into Scotland. Through England the escape routes were barred. In 1302 Bruce had married Elizabeth de Burgh, daughter of the Earl of Ulster. Through this alliance with Ireland he could keep open the sea routes from Ireland to Scotland. Quite possibly, the Templars could reach Scotland after circumnavigating Ireland to the west and north and landing on Bruce's domains of Argyll and Kintyre. [6]

Though speculative, the above thesis is based on compelling circumstantial evidence. What is known conclusively is the survival of the Templars as a separate entity in Scotland for another two centuries. We know, for example, that even in 1338 the Knights Hospitaliers of St John had still not taken possession of Templar lands. When they did, these were kept separate, as if in trust. At the end of the 16th century 519 sites in Scotland (579 according to another document) were listed as 'Terrae Templariae'. [7] We also hear Sir Walter Scott making reference to the Templars in a poem about the battle of Halidon Hill in 1333. In speaking to king Edward the Third of England, the knight Adam Vipont says: "….I was a Scotsman ere I was a Templar…" [8]

The Expedition

Was there really an early Scottish attempt to colonize America? If so, what were the results of such an effort? To answer these and other questions, we will have to look more closely at the St. Clair family (later Sinclair). Through their possessions in the Orkneys and at one time in the Shetlands, the St Clairs owed allegiance to Norway as well as Scotland. The people of the Orkney and the Shetland Islands were predominantly Norse. In 1379 the Norwegian king appointed Henry St. Clair as Earl of Orkney, in honor of his ancient Norman heritage and in spite of problems of possible conflict of allegiance between Scotland and Norway. While nominally dependent from the king of Norway this gave Henry a de facto independence, coupled with the ability to mint coin and the mandate of raising a navy to effectively control the islands of the dispersed archipelago, contended by Scots and Norwegians. As the only Earl of the kingdom of Norway, Henry was next in rank to the royal family; he had authority of elector to the three kingdoms of Norway, Sweden and Denmark. (9) From the above we realize that the St. Clair played a special role between Scotland and Norway, and disposed of considerable power and autonomy. This placed them in a particularly favorable position for an attempt to reach America. Geographically the Orkneys on the Northern tip of Scotland offered an ideal route to the New World and nearly complete isolation for any project wishing to maintain a high level of secrecy.

The Venetian Zeno family appears on the scene of the expedition through what appears to be a twist of fate. Frederick Pohl relates the story of the last minute rescue of Nicolo Zeno, shipwrecked on Fer Island (Shetland Islands). The island tradition made such a boat fair game for looters; the sailors would simply be massacred. Henry Sinclair, who happened to be on the island with his war ships, noticed a frantic group of people running toward the shore and managed to arrive on the scene in time to save the foreigners. (10) Thus, to all appearances the encounter of Nicolo Zeno with the Sinclair Earl was entirely fortuitous. One is left to wonder however, what a Venitian ship could have been doing so far from home. On the other hand we find that Carlo Zeno, Nicolo's brother, later became a Venetian ambassador to

France and England in 1396, while his brother was preparing a fleet for an American expedition. A concerted effort seems likely to have been present behind the expedition. In the past, the Zenos had formed ties with Vikings and Normans at the times of the crusades. The Venetians, like the Templars, provided shipping vessels for the fighters. (11)

The Sinclair-Zeno expedition is the only documented pre-Columbian landing in the New World. The maps and documents left by Antonio Zeno were later found by his great-great-great-grandson. The idea of the exploration seems to have come to Earl Henry as early as 1397, upon hearing the story of a fisherman driven by a storm upon the island then given the Viking name of Estotiland, (corresponding to modern day Newfoundland) where he spent five years. Henry, as Antonio recorded, decided to send a considerable number of vessels and men there, and to go personally instead of delegating the task to Antonio.

What the purpose of the expedition might have been we can only surmise. Yet all the circumstances seem to point in the same direction. We will first look at the evidence on American grounds. The expedition arrived in America on Trinity Sunday, June 2nd 1398. Trin Harbor, the place of their landing, has been identified by the historian Frederick Pohl as Chedabucto Bay. In the Pictou area of Nova Scotia the expedition started building a city in a place that is considered the best harbor of the region. In near proximity, Antonio recorded the phenomenon of smoke and fire proceeding from a natural spring of pitch, located next to the ocean shore. This place is known as modern day Stellarton in Nova Scotia. This area has vast deposits of pitch. It received its name from the so-called stellar coal, an oil coal that emits short bright flames like stars upon burning. Such natural phenomena are very rare. No others occur in the Northern continent close to the ocean. (12)

Other pieces of evidence could possibly be connected with these early explorers. The most intriguing of them is the Newport Tower in Rhode Island. The tower is a building of circular shape built upon eight columns, forming a nearly perfect circle and supporting eight Roman arches. No mention of its building is found in colonial records, but it appears in a text from the Public Records Office in London in 1632, seven years before the founding of Newport. The tower remains a mystery as to who built it, but there are a few pointers about its origin. Its architecture resembles European architecture of the 14th or earlier centuries. It is built in the manner of the round churches of the Templars, which copied the baptisteries of early Christendom. An example of it, built on the Orkney Islands, dates from the 12th century. F. Pohl, taking the Newport Tower's measurements, found that it is built using the Rhineland Norse foot (12.3543 English inches) introduced in Scandinavia in the 13th century. The diameter of the columns and the internal and external diameters of the circle correspond to multiples of this unit. (13) It may seem puzzling that this tower unites Templar motifs with Norse workmanship, but we have seen that the St. Clair, although Scottish, ruled over Norwegian territory, and it is to be expected that the settlers be of mixed origin. At the base of the tower, Bjorndal and Lovfald have found Norse runes that read "of the Bishop's stool", most likely meaning "cathedral church". What the tower most likely stands for is an unfinished church. As it stands it necessitated considerable manpower. This architectural feature is most likely what appears in the Verrazzano map of 1542, with the mention of 'Norman villa', at a site quite accurately corresponding to Newport. (14)

This is not the entire body of evidence. Later proof survived over time through maps made by experts of the times. A Dutch map called the Gemma Frisius-Mercator of 1537 indicates Labrador and next to it three flags containing a square cross surmounted by a foliate cross. Not only do these resemble the Templar cross, but the additional notation of 'terra per britannos inventi' (land discovered by the Britons) reinforces the point. Mercator's great map of 1569 correctly shows Estotiland (modern day Newfoundland) at the eastern end of Canada. At the mouth of the St Lawrence River the map places a monastic church building, another apparent reference to the city that Sinclair would have founded. All of the above proves that the Zeno map was believed to be correct more than a century later. (15)

If a first attempt to colonize America happened, why was it so short-lived? It is obvious that such endeavor had to be conducted with a certain level of secrecy. Secondly, it completely rested on the key role of the Earl of Orkney. In the year 1400 King Henry the Fourth of England invaded Scotland. Earl Henry died at the hands of marine raiders coming from East Anglia during the same year that he returned from America. The last four years of his life, corresponding to the time of the expedition, remain unaccounted for. His son, also called Henry, while accompanying James the Crown Prince of Scotland to France, was captured and taken prisoner in England for many years. This left the newly founded colonies completely isolated, and nothing is known of their later evolution. [16]

Were the Templars and others who had similar intentions trying to create a paradise on earth beyond the reach of Papal authority? If not an altogether proved hypothesis, it is nonetheless a very plausible one. Is this vision the one that reappears later in the centuries with the mysterious motto "Et in Arcadia Ego"? This motto, sometimes abbreviated AE, first appears in the 'Unicorn tapestries', now in possession of the Cloisters Museum in New York, and printed on the title pages of books written during the Elizabethan times. The three words are visible in a painting by Guercino of 1621 known as Et In Arcadia Ego. Two peasants in a bucolic landscape contemplate a skull lying over a tombstone. Underneath the skull is the motto. Is this contrast of death within the quiet of nature a veiled indication of a paradise on earth, where death exists? A second painting by Poussin named The Shepherds of Arcadia, painted around the years 1640-1642, shows shepherds around a tomb. It has the particularity of portraying the real tomb of Marie de Blanchefort, located in the French village of Rennes-le-Chateau. The tomb bears the entire motto "Et in Arcadia Ego." [17]

All of the above is in keeping with the zeal of the Templars. Their aim had been the Christianizing of Europe and the foundation of a new social order. We know that the father of Earl Henri Sinclair had died in Eastern Europe fighting for the Teutonic knights, who were then trying to carve out their own kingdom of heaven on earth in those lands that were beyond the control of the Pope. We also know that a region of the Canadian Northeastern Atlantic bears in effect the French name of Acadie. [18] Was this name given in memory of an old ideal, which gradually became veiled and obscured over time?

The Templar social striving at the root of the 14th century attempt in America would have to wait three more centuries and reappear in a wholly metamorphosed way. In the intervening time, Eastern

North America produced its own renewing social impulse, coming this time from a little known individuality who radically transformed Iroquois and Eastern American society.

Prophet in the Wilderness: Deganawidah and the Iroquois League

The American federal system of government was born in a place where federalism already had a long tradition. We have seen the Lenni Lenape federation and the part in it that the Tamanend ideal played for the colonists. We will later see the two confederacies that the early settlers found at their arrival: the Wampanoag confederation in Massachussets and the Powhatan confederacy in Virginia. Many other confederacies existed along the Atlantic coast of North America, whereas there were fewer on the western side of the continent. All of them had a semi-feudal character. The recognized Sachem or leader received tributes from the various tribes and pledges of allegiance as a sovereign king would receive from his vassals. In return, the vassals received protection against common enemies.

The Iroquois League represents a radical departure from all previous models. It is the first confederation of equal nations, which does not rest on the idea of monarchy. The Five Nations' Confederacy traces its origin to the historical legend of the White Roots of Peace. Some modern authors have claimed that the ideas put forth by the Iroquois served as a blueprint for the American Constitution. The proof brought forth regarding this is very eloquent but not conclusive. It rests primarily on Benjamin's Franklin relationship with the Five Nations and his knowledge of their traditions. Although the Iroquois League has a key influence upon the birth of the American federal system, it is obviously not the only one. The colonists also had a long tradition of compacts and constitutions hearkening back to Anglo-Saxon tradition. We need not invoke a link of strict causality between two such different societies as the Iroquois and the American. It is rather the Iroquois social outlook that lives and plunges its roots into the American Revolution and the Declaration of Independence. Therefore it is significant that Benjamin Franklin acknowledged it and later played such a prominent role in the formation of the American idea.

The Iroquois, as they were called by the French, occupied the northern portion of present-day New York State in a territory extending roughly between the Genesee and Hudson Rivers. They comprised the five tribes of Senecas, Cayugas, Onondagas, Oneidas and Mohawks. The symbol of their legend, the tree of the white roots, stands for *peace* in the broader sense of the word, a peace that in their language corresponds with Law, in other words sacred law.

The events related in the legend occurred between 1400 and 1500, most likely around 1450. The Wallam Olum indicates the Five Nations Iroquois, whom it calls Mengwe, for the first time in 1438. This may correspond to the date of the founding of the league. [(19)] Tamanend II, as we have seen in the previous chapter, may have been a contemporary of Hiawatha and Deganawidah.

There are many versions of this historical legend. [(20)] Variations can be attributed to the accuracy of the sources relating the events, the kind of witnesses recording them and the time of these recordings. Some versions are obviously shorter renderings trimmed of any legendary character and made fit for a more modern rational ear. Of all the versions known, we will mainly refer to Paul Wallace's retelling, taken at the turn of the 19th century from three different sources. Wallace is a thorough interpreter of Iroquois culture and is completely immersed in their way of thinking. We will occasionally use other sources to amplify Wallace's version.

The Legend of the White Roots of Peace

> Deganawidah, the central hero of the history, is born among the Huron, tribe of the north shore of the Lake Ontario. He is a foreigner in relation to the Five Nations. He is the son of a virgin and his name - meaning 'Master of Things' - has been revealed to the grandmother by an apparition of the Great Spirit. His declared mission is to bring peace and spread what he calls the 'New Mind' among the nations. He wants to turn his back to war and revenge and bring about a new law. Although an exalted being, Deganawidah has a stutter.

When Deganawidah grows to manhood he sets out toward the rising sun, riding in a white canoe made of stone, knowing that he will not return. He arrives on the southern shore in Iroquois territory, at that time ravaged by strife, and goes from one settlement to another spreading the word of peace. After visiting these, Deganawidah goes to the house of a woman 'who lived by the warrior's path which passed between the east and west.' To the woman Deganawidah recites the message of peace that he divides into three parts:

- righteousness, as the desire to see justice embodied
- health, meant as harmony of body and mind and a foundation for peace
- power, based on law that has the backing of force, but a force that translates the desire of the 'Holder of the Heavens'.

To the woman's question of which form this word would take in the world, Deganawidah foretells what would later be known as the Longhouse - the house of many fires - symbol of a confederacy of equals. The woman embraces the message and Deganawidah gives her the name Jigonhsasee, meaning the 'New Face that embodies the New Mind', and tells her that she would be remembered as 'Mother of Nations'.

Upon leaving the woman Deganawidah proceeds towards the sunrise, knowing that he will have to meet with 'the man who eats humans', in Onondaga territory. Arriving at the man's hut, Deganawidah climbs on the roof and stands waiting with his head next to the smoke hole. The man returns home with a corpse and sets the kettle over the fire. On the surface of the water he sees Deganawidah's face and he believes it to be his own reflection. Detecting in it a strength and wisdom that he has never surmised before, he starts questioning his cannibalistic habits. This change of mind brings him sorrow at the realization of the evil he has committed. Thus moved, he ponders what needs to be done in order to compensate for the pain he has caused. At that moment Deganawidah enters the hut, appearing to the stranger. The latter relates his experience and Deganawidah offers him the means of redressing his wrongs by explaining to him the 'Good News of Peace and Power'. From now on the cannibal will have the name of Hiawatha (which means 'He who combs'). At the same time he is given the task and challenge of enlisting the wizard Atotarho to their cause.

Atotarho, whose name means 'Entangled', is versed in the arts of magic. He has 'a twisted body and a twisted mind, and his hair is a mass of tangled snakes'. He strikes terror in his enemies and holds great power. His cry 'Hwe-do-ne-e-e-e-eh', meaning 'When shall this be?' is said to be 'the mocking cry of the doubter who killed men by destroying their faith'. He can strike his enemies even at great distances. Before setting Hiawatha on his new task, Deganawidah visits the wizard and announces to him the coming of the Good News of Peace and Power, without managing to sway his mind. Still proceeding towards the sunrise, he arrives among the last Iroquois tribe, the Mohawks. They are favorably inclined towards the message but want to receive a sign by testing the messenger. They ask the foreigner to climb a tree next to the lower falls of the Mohawk River. They fell the tree over the river and Deganawidah survives unscathed into the next day. This is the sign they desire and the Mohawks accept the prophet's message. They are the first nation to accept the New Mind.

In Onondaga territory Hiawatha spreads the new message without managing to loosen Atotarho's grip over his people's minds. Three times he calls a council and after each one of them one of his daughters is taken ill and dies, victim of the powers of Atotarho. Finally, the Onondagas arrange to have a game of Lacrosse performed to lift Hiawatha's spirits. During the game a mysterious bird comes down from heaven. The crowd pursuing it causes the death of Hiawatha's wife, who is trampled in the onrush. Unable to contain his grief, Hiawatha wanders away towards the east. He reaches one of the Tully Lakes where the ducks lift the water to leave him a dry passage. On the bottom of the lake he finds shells that he strings together with three ropes. These he sets on a horizontal pole supported by two vertical ones. Holding each string in turn, Hiawatha recites words of comfort that he pledges to repeat to anyone that mourns over a loss. This is the so-called Ritual of Condolence. In vain he waits for anybody to console him. After a few weeks of mourning, he arrives at the village by the Lower Falls of the Mohawk River. Here he reconnects with Deganawidah. The Master relieves him of his grief by using the very same Ritual of Condolence.

At this point Deganawidah and Hiawatha set out to complete their tasks by concretely envisioning the form that they want to give to their message of peace. One after another the tribes accept their

> message. The final obstacle is Atotarho. The two decide that Deganawidah will sing to him the Song of Peace, while Hiawatha will explain the Words of the Law. They set forth in a canoe across a lake to meet Atotarho. The wizard, using his last magic powers, sends winds and waves against the canoe, but to no avail. Deganawidah and Hiawatha thus bring their message to a skeptical but more receptive Atotarho. To accomplish the great reconciliation he has in mind, Deganawidah invests Atotarho with the highest authority over the Five Nations. In the presence of the Five Nations he tells Atotarho: 'Behold! Here is Power. These are the Five Nations. Their strength is greater than thy strength. But their voice shall be thy voice when thou speakest in council, and all men shall hear thee." Then Atotarho's mind is made straight and Hiawatha combs the snakes out of his hair. Deganawidah lays his hands on the wizard's body and removes the seven crooks. Then he places antlers on Atotarho's and the other chiefs' heads as a symbol of their new authority.

Let us now look at the implications of this legend and the historical facts that ensued. In the language of the legend, the 'New Mind' has to bring about a New Form. New ideas shape a new reality in the social world.

The Message and the Form

In most versions of the legend, Hiawatha and Deganawidah form a duality. Occasionally they merge into the single individuality of Hiawatha. The dynamic of the legend revolves around the two of them and Atotarho.

Deganawidah's biography is by far the most extraordinary of the three since he is conceived by a virgin. In some versions of the legend the messenger also prophesies that Deganawidah would indirectly bring the downfall of his people, the Hurons. The Grandmother tries to kill him by throwing him in the freezing waters and twice again in unspecified manners. [21]

In Deganawidah we see an initiate who tries to introduce new spiritual principles. That he is an initiate or an exceptional person is also indicated by the fact that he rides in a white canoe made of stone. In the version of the legend quoted above, once his mission is accomplished, Deganawidah rows in his canoe towards the setting sun, never to be seen again. In the version given by Horatio Hale it is also said that Deganawidah is the only name that cannot be used down through the line of heredity, contrary to that of all the other chiefs present at the foundation of the League. This is because none can do what he has done. [22]

Like Deganawidah, Atotarho (alternatively spelled: Thadodaho) shares a mixture of human and superhuman attributes. His cry is 'the mocking cry of the doubter who killed men by destroying their faith'. The translation of the cry means 'When will this be?' This impatient attitude is typical of a being who wants to bring forth events before their time. The physical appearance of Atotarho – his crooked body, his head covered with snakes - is the expression of the fact that he is a black magician.

Between these two extremes stands Hiawatha. His flaw, cannibalism, is a major trespass that he has inherited as a cultural habit. It is a practice tied to war and religious beliefs. Cannibalism stands at the center of the encounter between Hiawatha and Deganawidah. Because Hiawatha is in touch with his true humanity, he is able to overcome his cannibalistic habit. The prophet allows him to recognize his shortcomings and realize his full human potential. This brings about the recognition of the pain caused to others and the desire to redeem himself, made possible by Deganawidah's message.

Soon after, Hiawatha takes on the task of helping his people. The length of the process of grief is emphasized by the establishment of the Ritual of Condolence, the burdensome journey to the Mohawk nation and the earnest desire to bring consolation to others. Only Deganawidah knows the depth of Hiawatha's sorrow. He can reach to the spiritual source which offers him peace and allows for perception of the truth that suffering has obscured.

The dynamic of development played by the two founders shows significant nuances that could escape first sight. Hiawatha is as much a pupil of Deganawidah as he is a collaborator. While the prophet carries the vision he is also impaired by his stuttering. He needs someone else with oratorical skills; that is Hiawatha's role. Although Deganawidah guides and inspires, it is Hiawatha who carries out the burden of the central confrontation with Atotarho. He cannot make use of supernatural powers as Deganawidah does in the instance of the test of the fallen tree. Still, it is Hiawatha who establishes the Ritual of Condolence and who combs Atotarho's hair. The prophet has to find a willing companion before he can realize his mission. With the achievement of the League Deganawidah's task comes to an end. Hiawatha still has a political task to carry out.

The legend has still other implications on the social level. The Ritual of Condolence has a central place in Iroquois society, not immediately noticeable from the legend. Previous to the advent of the League the strife between the tribes was perpetuated by cycles of war and revenge, cannibalism and black magic. The cornerstone of Iroquois Society is the recognition of the need for the process of grief and consolation to replace the cycle of violence and revenge. The Ritual of Condolence makes possible the harmonization of the aims of the community by allowing individuals to overcome their grief and align their goals with those of others. Grief is seen as a veil covering the senses and the heart. The Ritual of Condolence lifts these veils and makes explicit the second principle expressed by Deganawidah: health as harmony between spirit and body.

More important still is the outcome of the legend in the form of government that arises within the Iroquois community. The New Word is the message of justice, health and power. The Iroquois know that a Word is nothing without a Form. They have embodied the Word in the Form of the Longhouse, symbolizing the union of many fires, which stood for the idea of confederacy. For the first time nations stand as equals, no more as vassals. Authority is defined by complex organizational levels built to ensure that no individual, nor single nation, can at any time impose their will upon the community. The political power is also clearly differentiated from the religious one. It is in fact a system of checks and balances, obliging the representatives of power to seek broad consensus in all their decisions. More detail about this form of government can be found in the fine analysis of Bruce Johansen. [23]

The Iroquois achievement is significant. It prepared a favorable ground in that part of the American continent where the American federal government saw its birth. We will now see how the Templar influence finally reached North America in a transformed way three centuries later.

The New Knighthood of Scotland

After Scotland's victory over England at Bannockburn, Robert de Bruce created two orders in which the Templars could find a haven: the Order of Scotland with the king as its Grand Master, and the Royal Grand Lodge of Heredom. The Sinclairs presided over the latter as hereditary 'Protectors of the King and the Crown Prince'. They also had jurisdiction over the Scottish Orders and Guilds, which they claimed the Templars had permeated with their rites and customs. [(24)]

William Sinclair, the architect of Rosslyn Chapel, near Edinburgh, was made 'Patron and Protector of the Scottish Masons' in 1440 by King James II of Scotland. [(25)] In 1600-1601 another Sinclair was confirmed the hereditary patron of the craft. That claim still held true in 1690. A later William Sinclair formally resigned from the inherited title to become the first elected Grand Master of the Scottish Freemasons in 1736. [(26)]

Dating from the 14th century we find the first document possibly pointing to the future Freemasonry: the so-called Kirkwall Teaching Scroll. It shows a depiction of Creation, and below it Paradise and the Angels. Further down we see the Temple of Solomon with the twin pillars of Jachin and Boaz. [(27)] Other documents mention the Old Charges and their use in the Crafts. These are legends, most likely orally preserved, that were to be recited at meetings - especially when new members were to be admitted. They trace the origin of the crafts, particularly masonry, to the time of King Solomon and the building of his temple. [(28)]

There is also evidence carved in stone in graves and tombstones everywhere in Central Scotland, between Edinburgh and the opposite coast, from the Counties of Fife and Lothian to the Mulls of Kyntire and Knapdale. In churches and graveyards we can see abundant evidence of Templar emblems (Templar crosses, floral and eight-pointed crosses, 'engrailed' octagons, knight effigies, swords, five- petaled roses, etc.) on some tombs. Other tombs carry Masonic symbols (mostly set squares, hammers, compasses), and intermediary stages show the co-existence of the various symbols. [29]

The first use of the word '*lodge*', or of the terms '*entered apprentice*' and '*fellow craft*' has also been registered in Scotland [30] Lodge was originally a temporary construction or a lean-to on the building site, where masons could eat, rest and meet. The term, which first applied to a building, evolved into the description of a working social group or an institution with its customs and rules. The transformation of the term 'lodge' perfectly illustrates the nature of the transformation undergone over time in the organization of Freemasonry itself. The Crafts and Guilds, still influenced by the Templars, slowly became the new entity of Freemasonry, gradually severing itself from the original entity.

The evolution of the Crafts into Freemasonry is emblematically portrayed in the Rosslyn chapel built by William Sinclair, the Third Earl of Orkney, in 1440. It can be called the last of the Gothic churches. It is the only one that hearkens back in spirit to the great cathedrals, although it is a pale image of their glory. We have seen that the village of Roslin, very close to Edinburgh, was associated with the miraculous spring of bitumen and oil used to cure ailments of the skin. Roslin occupies a remarkable place at the end of the Great North Road, also called Lactodorum (Milky Way), built by the Romans. This was the northern limit of Roman expansion. It is of some interest to know that while the village is spelled Roslin, the church is specifically called Rosslyn. Its possible Celtic meaning is knowledge passed down the generations. If so nothing could be more apt, for in Rosslyn we find many secrets engraved in stone.

William Sinclair must have been a very unusual and knowledgeable man to be able to personally design and direct the work of building Rosslyn instead of delegating the task, as was usual, to a Master of Works. A cross section of the building shows that it was built on the basis of the octagon, hexagon and triangles contained within the circle. The ground plan of the church matches what is known of Herod's Temple (built upon the old Solomon's Temple), particularly the placement of the walls and columns. The west wall of Rosslyn Chapel, believed to be a fragment of an unfinished cathedral, would be a replica of the ancient west wall of Herod's Palace, the only one that has survived destruction. This is now known as the 'wall of the lamentations'. Rosslyn's west wall seems to have been built independently of the rest of the building. Its stonework is not attached to any other existing structure and any attempt to build further against it would lead to a structural collapse. [31]

The nave has fourteen pillars, twelve matching and two uneven. The two pillars situated at Northeast and Southeast are different from each other and carved in richly ornamented designs; they represent Boaz, the Pillar of Strength, and Jachin, the Pillar of Wisdom, of Solomon's Temple. We can see that Sinclair had taken care to reconnect the church with an ancient tradition. Builders of the Gothic temples traced the origin and prototype of the cathedrals to the Temple of Solomon.

The interior walls are a true explosion of natural forms. For this reason the chapel has been called an 'herbal in stone'. Among the carvings is the story of Genesis, Adam and Eve chased from Paradise and an Angel with a flaming sword. A barrel-vaulted roof - unique in its kind and divided in five sections - represents the flowers of creation, culminating in the rose of Mary and merging into the stars of the firmament. To the south a Holy Dove is visible, flying with the Host in its beak. Below it is carved the symbol of the Grail, resembling a chalice or a crescent moon. Thus we have moved from the past, represented by Genesis, into the future suggested by the Grail. Could this floral extravaganza also be a pre-figuration of the Paradise sought on earth by the Templars - the new Arcadia? Among the sculpted plants there are two from the New World: maize and aloe. This confirms once again knowledge of America. Where could such specific knowledge come from, if not from a previous exploration? And what did Sinclair have in mind when he used these two plants in a building where nothing is strictly ornamental?

In more than one way Rosslyn chapel marks a turning point between the past and the future. A Latin inscription carved into an archway reads: "Wine is strong, a king is stronger, women are even stronger, but truth will conquer all." This is a motto later found in the Masonic ritual of the Babylonian Pass, previously believed to have originated in 1740. Another intriguing small carving shows a person initiating a candidate to a ritual, holding a noose around the latter's neck and a Templar cross on his chest. This represents once again what was thought to be a uniquely Masonic ceremony. [32] Elsewhere appears the carving of an eagle with two heads, known in Freemasonry as the Emperor of East and West, symbol of a Mason of the highest degree.

The above symbols need not be specifically Freemasonic symbols. They most likely are not, given the epoch in which the chapel was built. Rather, they prove the continuity between the Templar ritual with the Craft Orders and later with Freemasonry. In 1475, stone masons of Edinburgh were granted a charter of incorporation as a guild. When Freemasonry emerged in Scotland, it initially centered around a "lodge No 1", also known as Mary's Chapel. Interestingly, Saint Mary was the name under which the stonemasons of Edinburgh, then working at Rosslyn, were granted a charter of incorporation. [33]

Rosslyn chapel stands as a reminder of the past and a pointer towards the future. It looks back to the East, Palestine and the Temple of Solomon, and towards the future, towards the West and America. It also foreshadowed Freemasonry, which was soon to emerge. Once again the old Celtic West is intimately connected with the Northern American continent. As we will see the development of Freemasonry in America is closely bound up with its history in Scotland.

The later development of Freemasonry is intimately intertwined with the Scottish monarchy, the Stuarts in particular, and the English monarchy after the unification of the two kingdoms. In 1688 England, wanting to avoid the risk of a return to Catholicism through James II, offered the crown to James' anti-Catholic daughter and her husband William, Prince of Orange. The house of Orange (house of Hanover) had been Britain's arch-enemy a century before. The move left many wounds in the country. Although Scotland became part of England in 1689 without bloodshed, the Scots remained loyal to the House of Stuart, as did most of Freemasonry. The birth in 1717 of Grand Lodge was for all intents the attempt of the Hanoverian house to break the exclusive Stuart influence on Freemasonry. We need not be concerned by this schism, save for the fact that Scottish Masonry was the depositor of the true origin of Freemasonry and included the so-called higher grades, leading to the Royal Arch, and tended on the whole to be a less elitist movement. Nevertheless English Freemasonry, which erroneously claimed to be the first such movement, also played an important part in Freemasonry as a whole.

What then, was the role that Freemasonry played on the institutions and culture of the times? Previous to the installation of the Hanovers, the so-called "Invisible College' had been meeting in Oxford. From its efforts came the Royal Society in 1661. The membership of the latter overlapped considerably with Freemasonry. Grand Lodge on the other hand had a profound influence on the thought of the enlightened reformers of the 18th century: Hume, Locke, Voltaire, Diderot, Montesquieu, Rousseau. Some of them were Freemasons, while others partook of the prevailing Freemasonic ideas. Freemasonry acted upon society as a social solvent. In England it contributed greatly to the breakdown of the rigid social class system. For example, Jews were admitted into Freemasonry and public life in England earlier than elsewhere in Europe. Freemasonry also contributed to the distinction between man and office, so necessary to the development and furtherance of all democratic institutions. Finally, Freemasonry worked hand in hand with the Anglican Church in England and all the other churches of the New World. It was a social glue at a time when factionalism was on the rise both on the political and religious levels.

An important development of Freemasonry was its spreading throughout Ireland. There the early Scottish Masonry preserved aspects that had been lost in England. It was the Irish Lodges that granted charters to the so-called 'Field Lodges' of the British Army. Through these Freemasonry spread over to the New World. The division between Freemasonry of English origin and of Scottish origin was mirrored in America between the Moderns (English Freemasonry) and the Ancients (Scottish Freemasonry). The first Lodges were those of the Moderns. Philadelphia had its own St. John Lodge in 1730 to which Benjamin Franklin belonged. A humble printer, having no special claim by birth, Franklin had already become Grand Master. The Moderns started to decline around the 1740's, while the Ancients were on the rise. Philadelphia's first Ancient Lodge was formed in 1757. The difference between the two lay in the centralism expected by the English Lodge versus the broad independence maintained by the Scottish or Irish Lodges. Once formed these Lodges tended to lose contact with the sponsoring body. Scottish and Irish Freemasonry also relaxed the elitist requirements of admission.

Scottish Freemasonry had its first strong influence through the Field Lodges of the British Army in the French and Indian War of 1754-1760. These Lodges, while still mostly formed by the higher officers, allowed advancement regardless of grade or social status. Officer Guinet, while only a Lieutenant, was elected Grand Master of Canada.[(34)] The hierarchy of Freemasonry was a hierarchy of recognition due to a variety of interconnected social factors. It was through the Field Lodges that the ideas of the enlightened philosophers started to penetrate into American society.

The Ethos of Freemasonry

Together with rituals Freemasonry introduced a strong social ethic. This began with the rules of etiquette. These rules included the salute between members, the admission to the Lodge – which required unanimous agreement following scrutiny of the moral character of the candidate – and such seemingly mundane things as dining and singing together. Controversial topics were banned from the gatherings. All of the above may seem superficial behavior. However, it went much deeper than that. In effect a whole code of conduct - celebrating moral virtue and fraternal love - was promoted within the Brotherhood.

It may not at first be apparent how such values could derive from the Crafts. In order to perceive this we must look to the realm of morality. As long as the organization of labor in the Crafts survived, man's intimate connection with his vocation and the fruit of his labor also persisted. This connection would subsequently be lost with the dawn of the age of industrialization, which saw a progressive specialization and division of labor. With these changes came a separation between man and the fruits of his work.

All crafts required that the apprentice learn a large amount of specific gestures. The craft gesture is different from machine labor because it preserves the personal interaction of the worker with the material used. Through these particular gestures the crafts allowed a specific training of the will. The gesture had specific rhythms, which have to be gradually acquired and individualized. In its relationship with the craft material the self momentarily loses consciousness ofitself in the act of observation and interaction. The crafts raised simple motor activity to skill, willpower into beautiful form, and the simple gesture to the level of virtue. In this sense they deeply influenced human morality.

Doing the good, acting in the sphere of morality, this was the inheritance of the Crafts within Freemasonry. The relation to the craft materials and aims extended now to relationships within the fellowship. An equivalent relationship to the one existing towards the materials of the crafts applied in a metamorphosed way to human relationships. There were three things that the apprentice had to forego. These were: gratuitous curiosity, the fear to acknowledge his own failings and mistakes, and the inability to rise in spirit above all things which differentiate one human being from another. In this we see why Freemasonry could accept all religious and political ideas. Its universal tolerance enabled it to transcend and unite them in spirit.

The spirit of early Freemasonry, as it derived from the Crafts, is present within the Temple Legend and its historical background. There we see the Hebrew Solomon having to work with the Phoenician Hiram. Two representatives of two very different cultures are necessary in order to make the temple a reality. On the historical level the cooperation between Phoenicians and the Hebrews - referred to in many places of the Bible [35] - can serve as a model for working within the social realm. The Hebrews in effect received the revelations of sacred law, but lacked the skills for the building of the ambitious Temple, which Phoenicia could supply. Phoenicia in turn was dependent on Israel for wheat, barley, oil and wine. Israel depended on Phoenicia for its manufactured goods. At the time Phoenicia, a purely commercial state, had to rely for its existence on mercenary forces. The alliance with Israel and its large army allowed Phoenicia to expand trade. Phoenician commerce was made safe by the Hebrew military strength and so both parties benefited. A time of social prosperity resulted from the collaboration of these two distinctive nations.

Given the favorable religious and spiritual background Freemasonry played a role in America that it did not attain to in Europe, most particularly in France, where Freemasonry tended to become secularized. The strength of American Freemasonry was made possible by the social and spiritual climate that pervaded the colonies in the 18th century, a spirit quite different from its European counterpart. Even more so, it was brought about by the stature of some exceptional individuals. We have examined the individuality of Washington. Behind him looms even larger the figure of the nearly forgotten spiritual father of America, Benjamin Franklin. Through the complementary actions of these two towering individuals, the early Freemason ideal of Scotland and the Iroquois social renewal converged into a first tentative experiment of social art on a national level. These interlocking influences are embodied in the American form of government.

A New Look at the American Revolution

We will now analyze the process of the American Revolution and Independence, under the light shed by the previous examination of European and Native American influences weaving within the otherwise well-known events. We will focus on two levels. The first is the dynamic of the events, which shows how the Iroquois impulse was alive under the surface. Closer to the surface, but often misunderstood, is the contribution of early Freemasonry. Two extreme views hold the ground in this respect. One almost completely dismisses Freemasonry and tends to minimize, if not obliterate, its part in the events leading to the birth of the federal government. The other sees a mysterious, hidden Freemason conspiracy. Facts tend to prove something different from the two extremes. We will now shed light on little known and explored facts that reveal a somewhat different image of the familiar events.

Spreading the Message: Benjamin Franklin

We have already seen what a special position Franklin occupied in the scientific and spiritual thinking of the times. We can say he was a lone exception to the unavoidable tendency of the times that wanted science and religion to part ways. But Franklin's role wasn't limited to the depth of his thought. As early as 1764, he was appropriately called the 'First American'. [36] The term was later transferred to Washington.

It is easy to see why Washington, the man of action, could usurp the title. Even so, America was an idea before it became a political task, and in that sense the honor belongs to Franklin. We will have a look at the main aspects of Franklin's life before moving on to what his contribution was to the founding of the new nation.

Franklin, quite like Washington, had been groomed in the American school of business; but unlike Washington, his was an enterprise of the written word. His mission was to spread the word, not only in America but also to the world. By age forty-two, both men had reached prominent places in their societies, north and south. At that age they had achieved a high degree of economic independence and could devote their endeavors to the commonwealth.

Both Washington and Franklin had strong physical constitutions. However, Franklin - more than twenty years older than the Virginian - had a very different make-up. Whereas the young Washington towered in ambition, the young Franklin tended to naivete. His childhood friend, Collins, squandered the money that Franklin collected for Mr. Vernon and left the young man in debt. William Keith, governor of Pennsylvania, sent Franklin on a mission to London, and left him bereft of any support. In London the story repeated itself and James Ralph lived at Franklin's expense. This wasn't the last episode, but by then Franklin had learned the lesson; his amiability, brightness and constant striving towards self-improvement quickly compensated for other personality flaws.

Whereas Washington could bring the essence of the American experience within his reach through his enormous will, Franklin attained the same end through his traveling and his interactions with people and ideas. During his visit to France in 1767 he wrote to Polly Stevenson: "Travelling is one way of strengthening life, at least in appearance. It is but a fortnight since we left London, but the variety of scenes we have gone through makes it equal to six months living in one place. Perhaps I have suffered a greater change, too, in my person, than I could have done in six years at home."

In his early youth Franklin was already a leader among his peers in their games. He had a yearning towards the ocean that he associated with the idea of wanting to sail. In it we can see an intimation of his destiny that took him across the ocean to Europe. In his adolescent years he had unusual preoccupations with moral and spiritual matters, as he showed in his experiments with abstention from meat and alcohol. These were existential questions that the young man wanted to explore through his own experience. His transition into adulthood was fraught with many intense trials at around the age of twenty-one. In London he had contacted a group of young radical freethinkers and set out to prove "in a hundred axioms that he knew neither sin, nor liberty, nor personal immortality. God was only permitted to exist as a machine." He returned to Philadelphia feeling that he could have fallen into an abyss. Another abyss followed, one in which he almost lost his life after an attack of pleurisy. His friend and mentor, Denham, actually died from the illness they had contracted together. Of the depth of this experience we can gather some insight from his own words: "I suffered a good deal, gave up the point in my mind, and was rather disappointed when I found myself recovering; regretting in some degree that I must now some time or other have all that disagreable work to do over again." That Franklin gained a glimpse into the spiritual world seems beyond doubt. The next year he composed the famous epitaph, in which he said the following about his corpse: "…for it will (as he believ'd) Appear once More in a New and More Elegant Edition Revised and Corrected by the Author." This proves astonishing insights for a man of the eighteenth century, one coming from inner conviction rather than from borrowed knowledge. This was also the time in which Franklin formed the Junto. Even before becoming a Freemason four years later, Franklin started a group which shared much of its philosophy with the Brotherhood. His later affiliation with Freemasonry formed a thread throughout his life.

A glimpse at what Franklin's mind could encompass is truly astonishing. We can look first at speculative sciences. With little equipment and time dedicated to the matter, Franklin's discoveries about electricity are all the more remarkable. His insights endure today in the definition of positive and negative fields. More astonishing and little known is Franklin's mathematical genius. Through his friendship with James Logan, Franklin had become acquainted with the so-called 'mathematical magic squares'. These are square tables of eight columns by eight rows filled with seemingly random numbers. The sum of each column or row as well as the diagonals yield the same constant number. Not only could Franklin replicate such squares on his own; he could also add a host of additional constant properties to the 8 x 8 squares and also do the same with 16 x 16 squares. [37]

Thus Franklin's mind could have excelled in speculative pursuits. His achievements may seem less than the ones we just mentioned, but had an immediate benefit for his community and the whole of the colonies. With the press he worked his way into his fellow citizen's minds through Poor Richard's Almanac. The condensed wisdom, summed up in few words and peppered with humor, was particularly adapted to the ways of the New World. His declared intention was to: " ...leave a strong impression on the memory of young persons." [38] On the other hand, Franklin elaborated new ways towards knowledge, and put his mind to a myriad of practical applications in the social world.

His very approach towards knowledge is a radical departure from the ways of the academic world. His Leather Apron Club or Junto is the model of learning achieved in lively collaboration, the knowledge accessible to the leather apron man, - the craftsman, and by extension to all. Franklin understood that we learn from active interchange and life as much as from academic study. It is through the agency of the Junto that the Lending Library, the City Watch or the American Philosophical Society were born. About the improvements brought by the City Watch, Franklin said: "...by preparing the minds of the people for the change, it paved the way for the law obtained a few years later, when the members of our clubs were grown into more influence." Here we see another of Franklin's capacity, the one that early Freemasonry stressed: the ability to guide through deeds, deliberately relinquishing ownership of the ideas. This implies the willingness to plant a seed and wait for its fruition in a completely detached way. Not only was Franklin able and willing to abandon the paternity of his ideas, but he also knew when an idea had met its time and when it had to wait.

How much Franklin could achieve by turning to the practical and mundane may be encapsulated by taking the house as a symbol. On so many levels his ideas contributed to a better livelihood. The so-called Franklin stove allowed a more efficient use of wood. The lightning rod protected the home from a major source of fires. Moving on to a larger scale, Franklin and his Junto were instrumental in bringing about the Union Fire Company. The mature entrepreneur could formulate sixteen years later the revolutionary idea of the Union Fire Insurance Company, allowing the extension of the services of the Union Fire Company to reach a much larger part of the population.

It wasn't just Franklin's ideas that had a pervasive influence among the colonies. His tasks as Postmaster for Philadelphia, and later as deputy Postmaster General for the colonies, allowed him to cover a large territory. By age forty-two Franklin had achieved economic independence. He was also the Grand Master of Pennsylvania Freemasons. In his own world he had greatly contributed in holding a balance between the Quaker proprietors and the other forces of society, including the Freemasons. His presence was a key factor in defusing all tensions between centrifugal tendencies.

In the next twenty years his views expanded. He gradually became a man of the British Empire and a man of the world. His youthful wanderings in London had already played an important role in his education. In London, exposed to a rich cultural life, he came to see himself as a man of the British Empire. In his articles of belief at age twenty-two he had written: "...that I may be loyal to my Prince and faithful to my country, careful for its good, valiant in its defense, and obedient to its Laws, abhorring Treason as much as Tyranny."

With good reason was Franklin called 'the First American' before such honor fell upon Washington's shoulders. The idea of America - what made it different from any nation until that time - matured in Franklin's mind. It is easy to underestimate Franklin's achievements because he lived in a world of ideas and personal relationships rather than heroic deeds. He was a man of peace, whom some have called a 'reluctant incendiary'. It must also be kept in mind that he wasn't at liberty to speak his mind candidly. He often had to veil his words or hide them under the subterfuge of a convenient pen-name. That he could at all speak his mind was due to his reputation as scientist and philosopher and the popularity that preceded him wherever he would go. We can retrace the steps that Franklin took in spirit, and how they anticipated as if in a blueprint everything that later took shape in the world.

The first London exposure and the return to Philadelphia showed young Benjamin the disparity between the ideas of a cosmopolitan culture and the reality of Empire on the economic level, one that he couldn't fail to notice from the vantage point of the world of business. As early as 1747, the colonies' agent to London was advocating freedom of trade among the colonies. The first direct criticisms of British imperialism and mercantilism appear in 1751 in the Observations Concerning the Increase of Mankind, Peopling of the Countries,.... Here, in a yet timid way he was advising caution: "...Britain should not too much restrain manufactures in her colonies." He is more pointed on the topic of slavery: "The labour of slaves can never be so cheap here as the labor of working men in Britain."

The year that marked the emergence of Franklin on the continental scene, 1754, with the Treaty of Albany, was also a turning point for his thinking in economic matters. To Governor Shirley he outlined the burdens that the Americans carried from the prevailing practice of Empire. He complained of the amount of indirect English taxes that the colonists had to pay, i. e. the taxes incorporated in the English goods they imported. He perceived likewise the economic loss derived from enforced monopolistic purchases from and sales to England - given the preclusion from other competitive markets. All of these impositions were in fact, as he claimed, additional unspoken taxes paid to England.

But Franklin realized that the major obstacle to whatever small union between the colonies existed first and foremost in their own internal rivalries. Already in 1751 to James Parker, referring to the Iroquois he had written: "

> *" It would be a very strange thing if Six Nations of Ignorant Savages should be capable of forming a Scheme for such an Union and be able to execute it in such a manner, as that it has subsisted Ages, and appears indissoluble, and yet a like Union should be impracticable for ten or a dozen colonies."*

By 1764, in what he could express privately to Peter Collinson, Franklin's views had evolved to a point hardly reconcilable with the prevailing English economic interests.

> *"In time perhaps mankind may be wise enough to let trade take its own course, find its own proportions, etc. At present, most of the edicts of*

princes, placaerts, laws, and ordinances of kingdoms and states for that purpose prove political blunders. The advantages they produce, not being general to the commonwealth, but particular to private persons or bodies in the state who procured them, and at the expense of the rest of the people."

Yet, for Franklin there was nothing economic that wasn't a reflection of a human and moral dilemma. In the same letter he wrote: " I think there is scarce anything you can do that may be hurtful to us but what will be as much or more so to you." What was true of human relations in general was all the more true of nations, no matter how it was expressed or disguised under codified economic relationships.

We have seen that Franklin was a man of the Empire at first. However, his was an Empire other than British imperialism could tolerate. It was an Empire of equal parts under one king. In it there could be no economic privileges sanctioned by political charter. The new politician clearly expressed this in 1754, at the Treaty of Albany. His <u>Plan for Settling Two Western Colonies</u> was a last-ditch effort to implement a larger Empire of equals. Had his efforts been heeded, the War of Independence could have been averted.

Over time Franklin came to realize how entrenched were the commercial and economic interests intimately intertwined with Crown and Parliament. All of those he denounced cleverly or sarcastically at turn, often operating in disguise under cover of a pen- name. The variety of articles, essays and pamphlets culminated in <u>An Edict of the King of Prussia</u>.... and <u>Rules by Which A Great Empire</u>.... The second in particular, written in 1773, can be considered a forerunner of the Declaration of Independence. In it were listed in twenty points the grievances of the colonists against the mother country. Franklin advised prudence but stood firm for American rights. Thus, it was only natural that he would assume a central role in the Continental Congress and the drafting of the Declaration of Independence. Behind the scenes he had walked in spirit the steps leading to independence.

Franklin's idea of America evolved from a larger universal idea of Empire. It was almost a world federation before it turned by necessity into a specifically American federal system. The idea of the union of different parts - a sort of world brotherhood - emanated from Franklin's lifelong involvement with Freemasonry. After all his spiritual brethren stretched to both sides of the ocean, as Franklin's later participation in French Freemasonry proved.

It was as a man of the world-at-large that Franklin promoted the idea of America in Europe. The American diplomat knew that if America were to become a new phenomenon in the world, it had to overcome deeply engrained cultural habits. While at home Washington was devising new ways to fight a war of education, Franklin was fighting the diplomatic war that could win America's independence. He knew that he had to win over the French people. He also knew that he had to inaugurate a new era in international relations by trying to move away from political alliances and entanglements. He chose to focus on the arena of economic reciprocity - clearly stated mutual advantages, rather than the delicate balances of power at the mercy of a volatile political climate. In order to achieve this goal he had to prevail over others such as Lee and Adams who still operated within the old frame of mind.

Franklin's career reached its summit at the Constitutional Convention. Three events may symbolize the impact of his presence. His was the proposal of Washington for president of the Convention, a major step in creating consensus. Franklin, as the eldest man, stood tall for his wisdom. It wasn't his ideas which won the delegates over, (they were often in the minority) but rather his faith in the future and his ability to reach fruitful compromises. Under this light his call to prayer acquires a role much greater than symbolic. So does his call to the delegates to rally to the new proposed constitution in spite of its imperfections, perceived or real.

A last aspect of Franklin's political life, worth mentioning here, concerns his relationships with the Native Americans. In 1736 he had already published his first account of a peace treaty with the Indians. During the next twenty-six years he published the accounts of another thirteen of them. In the early 1750's he became an Indian Commissioner for Pennsylvania. He was surely familiar with the idea of federal union that Canassatego and other Indian chiefs advanced for the colonies. During the debate leading to the Treaty of 1744, the Iroquois chief Canassatego had closed his speech with the following words:

" Our wise forefathers established union and amity between the Five Nations. This has made us formidable. This has given us great weight and authority with our neighboring Nations. We are a powerful Confederacy and by your observing the same methods our wise forefathers have taken, you will acquire much strength and power; therefore, whatever befalls you, do not fall out with one another." (39)

Franklin was probably defeated in his campaign for the Pennsylvania Assembly for defending Indian rights during the episode of the Paxton massacre, after which he wrote the impassioned text: A narrative of the Late Massacres in Lancaster County of a Number of Indians, Friends of this Province by Persons Unknown.

Consciousness and Grief

A single individual had walked ahead of his people to wrest from the world of ideas a clear understanding of the existing reality as well as of possible alternatives to it. He had to wait from the time of 1754, with the Treaty of Albany, until a second chance presented itself in 1776.

The Declaration of Independence marked a watershed in the history of consciousness in North America. The colonists had acquired an understanding of the grievances that weighed on them; they could name the adversarial force and recognize it. This allowed them to overcome their differences. The core of the Declaration is in the first few sentences. In recognizing the divine origin of human beings, it acknowledged the higher self of the individual that makes it worthy and able to govern itself. Since all men are innately equal, they must have equal rights and be subjected to the same law. Implicitly the law is there to curb the unrestrained instincts and to protect society.

The Declaration was not the product of Jefferson alone. Franklin and Adams had a part in revising it. The delegates of the states had to debate on it for three days and agree to it in varying degrees, although finally making a show of unity. Once again Franklin had a very important part in a decisive step. While he was signing the Declaration, Washington was already successfully commanding the Continental Army. It was Franklin who drew up the declaration giving Washington command of the army. Here we see already highlighted the polarity between the two men. Franklin travels through the world,

Washington never leaves American soil. While their life-paths seldom cross, there is a mutual, implicit recognition of one another.

During the low point of the war, in 1780, Washington knew that his destiny lay with Franklin; he wrote to him acknowledging that the only possible choice lay between either peace with Britain or financial support from France. [40] Seven years later, Franklin knew that proposing Washington as the president of the Constitutional Convention was a way to establish it on a firm ground of trust and consensus. And in 1793, at the inauguration of the presidency, Franklin offered the crab-tree walking stick to the 'friend of mankind'.

Once the message had been spread, the commitment was going to be tested. The colonists, having recognized evil by its name, now had to face it. What Washington did was unique for a commander-in-chief in his time. He conducted a war of education, the education towards a new way of conceiving human relationships. It was education that was in effect to supply the motivation to a mostly unprofessional army. This, Washington accomplished on many levels. In the Army he strove to dissolve attachments to each particular colony. The field lodges served that purpose, mostly but not exclusively, among the officers. Freemasonry, interestingly enough, ended-up split on both sides of the Revolution - among the Republicans as well as among the Loyalists. Nevertheless, a larger part of the Ancients sided with the Revolution. Freemasonry, in effect, went on to play a larger role, as we will see later on. The universal appeal of the brotherhood attracted Von Steuben, De Kalb, Pulaski, Lafayette and others who left their country to rally to the American cause. For the soldiers, Washington requested the chaplains to call for prayers every day. On every account the commander knew that he needed to receive help from the spiritual world.

Furthermore, Washington agreed to work in concert with a Congress visibly weak and internally divided. This caused painful delays to his military campaigns and imposed hardships on the army. His task was more difficult than that which a high officer faced in a conventional army. He had to overcome the temptation to use his charisma in order to ease his situation. This would have hindered the very cause for which he was fighting. Working to educate rather than to lead also meant giving the benefit of the doubt and offering another chance to troublesome officers, as well as foregoing retaliation in order to promote unity.

The above facts are generally well-known aspects of the Revolutionary War. Other less known facts played an important role towards the resolution of the hostilities. The war was a painful civil war in more than one way. What caused Britain to fight against the colonies often stood in contrast with the soldiers' conscience in the field. Freemasonry' ideas crossed war lines. The opponents were literally spiritual brothers at war with each other. When de Kalb, mortally wounded, was found by Francis Rawdon, Cornwallis' second-in –command, the latter looked after him personally for three days. At his death a Freemason ritual was performed. Accounts abound of troops on either side capturing Freemason regalia and returning them to the enemy. When the warrant of the Leicestershire Regiment was captured, Samuel Parsons returned it with these words:

> "*. . . When the ambition of monarchs, or the jarring interests of contending States, call forth their subjects to war, as Masons we are disarmed of that resentment which stimulates to undistinguished desolation, and, however our political sentiments may impel us in the public dispute, we are still Brethren, and (our professional duty apart) ought to promote the happiness and advance the weal of each other.*" [41]

This certainly implied a delicate balancing act on both sides of the conflict. The split between duty and spiritual allegiance lived in the higher echelons of the British Army. The obvious choice for leading the British Army was Lord Jeffrey Amherst, a Freemason. He declined twice, the second time after George III had appointed him Commander-in-Chief in America. There is ample evidence indicating that Howe and Cornwallis were also Masons. Twenty-nine of the thirty-one regiments that Howe led had warranted Field Lodges. Howe went so far in expressing his feelings as to declare the colonists the 'most oppressed and distressed people on earth'. [42] It seems small wonder in the light of the above that he squandered precious opportunities to press the Continental Army in its moments of debacle during the initial phase of the Revolution. Isn't it surprising that Howe, after occupying Philadelphia, failed to exploit his superiority against the Continentals entrenched so close at hand at Valley Forge? Was Howe relieved at Yorktown, while his troops played the tune

'The World Turned Upside Down'? We may never know for sure. However, from all the above it is easy to surmise that ideas played a much larger role than usually credited in a place and time where history looks primarily at military strategy.

Another painful wound was awakened by the Revolution: the issue of slavery. We can see how this confrontation lived in Washington. The Virginian, like many others, was the carrier of a guilt similar to the cannibalism of Hiawatha, a cultural condition inherited from birth. It was in the years of the war that he was first shocked to see free Blacks fighting in the New England army. Soon after, he was promoting desegregation of the African Americans in the Rhode Island contingents. One cannot help but wonder at the further impact of the meeting with Phyllis Wheatley, the ex-slave turned poet, who dedicated a poem to the commander. Washington reports being impressed by her presence. However, he could not fully address the problem of slavery within the war.

The way in which Washington tackled the problem of slavery showed that he could penetrate to its depths, which were in the economic realm, before being political. By the end of his life, Washington had become a true pioneer in the field of agricultural practices. Having moved away from mono-culture, crops underwent a seven-year rotation plan. Plow-land was systematically returned to grass, manure was treated with utmost care and the soil was carefully fertilized. Every measure was applied to control erosion. All in all we see a model tending towards the best of present-day organic farming. Washington had truly attained a model of economic self-reliance and preservation of the environment. What Washington had achieved spoke as an answer for the woes of the Southern economy. Tobacco or cotton mono-cultures were not only humanly degrading to the slaves; they are also ecologically devastating. Washington could have left no better testimonial than his farms. He followed up his agricultural testament by freeing his slaves. He was thereby showing that the human solution to the problem of slavery had to follow the shift to a different economic approach. His decision of freeing the slaves at the end of his life was a symbolic one amidst the pervasive social forces that stood against it.

Even in this instance Washington pointed the way to the goal with his personal example.

The New Form of Government

The war had been a necessary step for the dissolution of the old social structures. The same centrifugal forces carried further would have made the nation vulnerable to foreign political and economic interests. A new political structure was necessary. When the need was finally felt, the Constitutional Convention gathered in Philadelphia. It only served an advisory function and many doubted it could have any impact. The Declaration had inaugurated new cultural ground, but the convention had an eminently political and practical scope. It could not reach as high in a practical way as the Declaration had set out to do. Therefore compromise was needed.

The distances to be bridged were often enormous: small states versus large states, pro-slavery against abolitionists, moneyed and speculative interests against demagogic tendencies, scholars and men of vision against men pursuing strictly local political interest. There were no clearly drawn lines, nor two defined sides. Every delegate had his own mix of issues.

What mostly held the convention together was in the first place the fame and stature of many of its participants. Washington played a central role by virtue of the fact that two thirds of the delegates had links of destiny with him, and by virtue of the role he played in the revolutionary war and in political office before that. His role condemned him to silence. His integrity standing beyond doubt, Washington seemed to be able to draw the best out of each person with whom he came in contact. Franklin was the oldest and one who could hardly be suspected of harboring partisan interests. His wisdom played a great part, together with his humor and his ability to defuse tension.

We will only look here at how the proceedings were conducted. In this lies the secret of their success. In the accounts of the four months of proceedings there is hardly any mention of emotional outbursts, all the more remarkable for a convention conducted in the summer heat of Philadelphia. The rules of listening had been so carefully laid out that it was not considered possible for any delegate to occupy himself with foreign matter, interrupt or in any way distract any speaker. To place things in perspective, some speakers held the floor for six hours.

The convention considered matters at hand as if it weren't faced by any practical limit of time. Issues were discussed for days and weeks. The delegates were truly meeting like their Iroquois counterparts, being used to discuss issues until unanimity could be reached. After such process had arrived at a certain stage, mandate groups were chosen in order to draft propositions and plans. More important than the allowance for time was the allowance for reconsideration. Delegates were given a chance and even encouraged to reconsider their opinions. A decision already taken and voted upon could still be reconsidered. Franklin's opinion on this account is worth quoting in full:

> *" We are sent here to consult, not to contend with each other; declarations of a fixed opinion, and of determined resolution never to change it, neither enlighten nor convince us. Positiveness and warmth on one side, naturally beget their like on the other; (and tend to create and augment division in a great concern), wherein harmony and union are extremely necessary to give weight to our councils, and render them effectual in promoting and securing the common good."*

In times of embarrassing silence, Franklin would invite the delegates to 'speak their sentiments'. Various delegates went from opposition to active support for the constitution. Some of the major instigators of the idea, like Randolph, finally came out against it. Many endorsed it in spite of their objections because they saw in it the best possible outcome for such an effort. Others, like Mc Henry, assented on the weight of the respect they held for the individualities assembled.

In all of the above, the best of Freemason practice and code of conduct prevailed. The convention acted truly as a brotherhood. Opposition wasn't simply tolerated, but fully received and considered. This allowed it to play a role in the further development of events. Washington summed up to Lafayette the feeling that a 'Whitsun event' had occurred where the result of the whole had become larger than what the sum of the participants could have achieved.

> *" It appears to me, then little short of a miracle that the delegates from so many different States, (which States you know are also different from each*

other) in their manners, circumstances, and prejudices, should unite in forming a system of national Government, so little liable to well founded objections."

In the preamble to the Constitution we see the famous 'We the People'. The constitution was in effect submitted to the People, not to the State delegates. Franklin had previously expressed this need in the following words:

"To get the bad customs of a country changed, and new ones, though better, introduced, it is necessary first to remove the prejudices of the people, enlighten their ignorance, and convince them that their interests will be promoted by the proposed changes; and this is not the work of one day."

This was the extension of the ideas of the Junto on a national level. The months following the convention were those of the largest endeavor of political education on a national scale ever witnessed up to that point, and probably ever since. It was a political exercise of high quality, involving qualified orators and eager popular participation. The ratification process took ten months, longer than the convention itself. The process of education and the active opposition to the constitution were sources of improvement to the final document. Provisions that had been fought against, or had been thought self-evident, were now incorporated into the Bill of Rights. Many who hadn't favored the initial document could finally accept the amended version. Others, who remained opponents, felt that they still had the chance to contribute to further improvements. Once the result was achieved many opponents felt they could rally the majority. Overall there weren't strong dividing lines between losers and winners.

On September 18, 1793, the United States Capitol was dedicated by Washington, dressed in Masonic apron. The silver plate placed upon the cornerstone indicated the 13th year of American independence and the year 5793 of Masonry. Washington and his brethren, all in ritual vestments, covered the cornerstone with the symbols of corn, oil and wine, Masonic representations of nourishment, refreshment and joy. There couldn't be a more explicit association of the ideals of the Republic with those held at the time by Freemasonry, by no less than the Chief Executive of the nation. Likewise Washington's often misunderstood effort as president to repudiate party politics was not an unrealistic utopian dream. It simply was the practice of the

Lodge, and could not be attributed to naivete in a man as shrewd and realistic as the president was.

From the above, the role of Freemasonry has emerged more fully. There is no need to envision a Masonic conspiracy when we see how pervasive its moral code was throughout the processes of deliberation of either Declaration, Constitutional Convention or ratification. Numerous actual Masons took part in the events; still more pervasive was the spirit that the Brotherhood promoted. We have also seen that it had a moderating influence on the events of the war.

In this presentation, we have only emphasized certain little known parts in order to make more visible the parallels between the Iroquois legend of the White Roots of Peace and the forming of the American federal system of government. Franklin and Washington play parallel roles to Deganawidah and Hiawatha. Also, the major steps of the process repeat themselves: acceptance of a message and its proclamation, trial and process of grief, overcoming and transformation of the evil fought against and new social form coming to birth. There seems in effect to be an inner necessity to this dynamic of how ideas seek manifestation in the social realm.

Fourth of July, Fourteenth of July: Two Revolutions

Fourth of July in America, Fourteenth of July in France - Independence Day and Bastille Day - these are the two events marking the beginning of the respective revolutionary outbreaks.

The French Revolution started on July 14th 1789, with an event markedly different from the Declaration of Independence. The storming of the Bastille was an insurrection reflecting the utter despair of the French people. To them the hated Bastille fortress symbolized tyranny and oppression. This act of revolt was followed by violence and later by the famous Reign of Terror. All of it was reflected in the philosophy of the Declaration of the Rights of Man and Citizen of August 27, 1789. In it the divine principle is mentioned only once. In later documents it is never mentioned again. The preamble states that the document is a "solemn declaration of the natural, inalienable rights of man'. The constitution of 1791 stated: "The law no longer recognizes religious vows or any obligation contrary to natural rights of the Constitution". The third constitution of Robespierre said on article 9: "Every citizen owes his services to the Motherland, and to the maintenance of liberty, equality and property, whenever the law summons him to defend them." Already from the first document, and all the more so with the succeeding ones, the human being had been divorced from all connection to the spiritual world, subordinated to the State and elevated at most to the rank of 'citizen'. Napoleon's dictatorship was the necessary outcome of a spiraling cycle of violence, as Schiller had predicted. His self-crowning stands in stark contrast to Washington's refusal of the crown.

In France too Freemasonry had advanced powerful ideas. Hers was the call to Liberty, Equality and Fraternity. Nevertheless the brotherhood had lost its vigor, that vital link with the world of spirit that inspires the youthful energy capable of bringing about social changes. Its internal weaknesses, as well as the opposing forces, brought about a completely different outcome. Anticlericalism, perfectly understandable in light of the place and role of the church, became almost a rage against every spiritual idea. With Napoleon, nationalism and the cult of personality were practically all that remained of the initial impetus of the French Revolution.

In America, through the consciousness infused into the Declaration of Independence and all the subsequent steps leading to the ratification of the Constitution, moral forces were consciously mastered and put to the service of the social compact. All emotionalism and gratuitous outbursts of violence had been carefully avoided to a high degree. Spiritual forces had truly brought about a very tangible renewal of society.

Chapter 4

Spiritual Movements in the 19th Century

" The soul has wants which must be satisfied; and whatever pains are taken to divert it from itself, it soon grows weary, restless and disquieted amid the enjoyments of sense."

(Democracy in America, Alexis de Tocqueville)

The 19th century marked important changes in human consciousness with the spread of the scientific outlook. It was the century that further introduced materialism in every area of life. In America, more than elsewhere, a certain restlessness set in, giving birth to its own manifestations through the interaction of organized religion and social activism. As we have seen, these were closely intertwined in the previous century.

The tendencies of the previous century manifested at times in a very dramatic way. Rationalism had its strongest embodiment in Unitarianism, founded in 1819, when it broke off from the Congregational Church. In it were compressed under a religious umbrella all the philosophical and political ideas of the English and French philosophers. Unitarianism has been called the 'democracy of religions'. Its creed was expressed by Al Channing: "The adoration of goodness, this is religion." What often united the Unitarians was their rejection of dogma from all other faiths. Overall they had little success in creating an organized structure and following for their rationalistic outlook.

At the time the movement known as the Great Awakening was resurfacing in Revivalism. The first wave hit North Carolina, Virginia and Maryland in 1787, another one spread through Kentucky and Tennessee in 1799. In the 1820's what was later known as the Great Revival swept through Western New York and the Upper Mid-West. Numerous other revivals burst like wildfires throughout the century. Nothing could characterize the dramatic extremes of the new conversion experience better than the 'exercises' - manifestations of physical emotional outbursts and frenzy. In the 'jerking exercises' the peak of religious ecstasy was reached through physical convulsions, sometimes accompanied by outspoken verbalism. In the 'barking exercise' people would drop onto all fours and bark, then run in packs to trees like dogs 'treeing' an opossum. Many of these physical exercises were meant to induce visions and trances. De Tocqueville, shocked, attributed these practices to extreme swings between a pronounced materialistic pursuit of welfare, and the balancing attempt to satisfy the soul's hunger for spiritual experience. His observation finds confirmation in the fact that individuals could move with relative ease between the two extremes of evangelism and liberalism.

We have seen how the changing times called forth this accentuation of polarities. Elsewhere this restlessness of mind and will gave way to what we may call a 'prophetic' mood. Here the term prophetic does not necessarily mean objective prophecy; rather it corresponds to a foreboding of a need for change. As was the case in the previous century, religious and political ideas overlapped. Even patriotism became imbued with prophetic religious overtones. We can see this tendency in the hymns: America, My Country 'tis of Thee, The Battle Hymn of the Republic, God of Our Fathers, America the Beautiful. Sarah Hale, the promoter of Thanksgiving, acted out of such a prophetic mood. On a large scale this foreboding mood became apocalyptic Millennialism. Such was the element weaving through the Millerite movement, which interpreted the coming age as the time of the Final Judgement and predicted the end of the world by 1844. Even without reaching the million followers which it claimed, it certainly was a movement of considerable dimension.

In the political arena and closely allied with religious fervor, appeared many differing reform movements such as: prison reform, improved treatment of the insane, women's rights and the peace movement. The entire spectrum of religious denominations participated in these pursuits. Mainly from organized religion came the formation of utopian communities. Most successful among them were the Shakers and the Mormons. Even the Transcendentalists had their own community at Brook Farm. These religious movements were far more successful than their political counterparts which included the North American Phalanx (Pennsylvania and New Jersey), Etienne Cabet's Icaria (Texas) and Robert Owen's New Harmony (Indiana).

Freemasonry evolved likewise in a parallel direction, symptomatic of the times. On one hand, with the establishment of Lodge Charity Funds and Boards of Relief, the brotherhood's commitment to the community focused specifically on charity. On the other hand, a complete redefinition of ritual was undertaken. The aim was to unify rituals that had tended to become heterogeneous, strengthening the meaning of symbols and ceremonies. This was a legitimate aim for an institution that was progressively losing a living connection between the symbols and their meanings. It was also undertaken with deep earnestness. However, it is very questionable whether this emphasis on ritual could really help renew the brotherhood.

The lodges appointed traveling lecturers to spread new unified versions of the rituals. These new ceremonies sought to stir the feelings and emotions. It was believed that the self had to be shaken before it could be re-established on better grounds. New rituals could last for hours and often required elaborate sets and props. The 'Knight Templar Ritual' depicted the death and resurrection of Christ and the knight's elevation to the role of apostle. Twelve lit candles arranged in a triangle represented the twelve disciples. The candidate would blow out a candle to symbolize Judas' betrayal. He would then wander as a 'pilgrim penitent' to whom were shown scenes of Jesus's death and resurrection. At the end of the ceremony, the candle was lit anew to indicate that the knight could now take Judas Iscariot's place in the circle of the disciples. (1) While these new rituals were based on the understanding that the individual needed to be stirred to vigorous activity, the emphasis on the feelings could only accentuate the tension of the soul that existed between Revivalism and Rationalism – emotionalism and dry intellectual detachment.

The 'Winged' Franklin

As Franklin had done in his time, Transcendentalism endeavored to pioneer a new way of approaching knowledge of the spiritual world. The new philosophy went further than Franklin had done. Transcendentalism's major representative, Emerson, had left the Unitarian ranks dissatisfied. In his approach he denied not only dogma, as the Unitarians did, but also rationalism. His circle drew inspirations from the German philosophical idealism, literary Romanticism and the Greek philosophers - among others. Emerson had also immersed himself in the sacred texts of world religions, particularly Eastern ones. This vast gamut of inspirational sources shows how much the Transcendentalists were experimenters of the inner path.

Emerson speaks of 'spiritual instincts'. These he qualifies as tools for knowledge in the following way: "You first have an instinct, then an opinion, then knowledge, as a plant has root, bud and fruit. Trust the instinct though you can render no reason. It is vain to hurry it. By trusting to the end it shall ripen into truth and you shall know what you believe" (From Intellect) From these lines we can also sense what Emerson draws from the scientific Goethe, with whose works he was completely familiar. His was a new way to reconcile faith and science - the inspiration he drew from the East - with the modern Western way of thinking. Along this path, the logical thinking of the West could rise to what he called 'intuitive thinking'.

Emerson was completely inspired by the spirit of the time. He knew that humanity was reaching a new watershed and that new faculties of perception into the spiritual world would arise. He expresses himself thus: "When those will arise who know about the true standard of values, the determination of value of the common marks of honour will sink down to the stand of cooks and confectioners. The genius is the scientist or geographer for the supersensible regions and will design a map of the new supersensible areas. But we, who become acquainted thereby with new areas of creation, lost something of our former admiration" (Representative Men).

Emerson was the herald of a new understanding of destiny, one that is no longer taken out of the traditions of the East, but needs to be awakened within the self. He knew that destiny has its origin within man. He sensed that there is a keen relationship between the individual and what occurs within his environment. Everything that happens to the individual corresponds to his inner needs; it fits the purpose of his inner evolution. Man has shaped his destiny in concert with higher beings and this knowledge will serve to give him strength and resolve in life.

The paradox of Emerson's way between East and West is what the poet Oliver Wendell Holmes captured in his description of Emerson, in a poem dedicated to the 'Saturday Club' - of which both were members. The following is a stanza from it:

"Where in the realm of thoughts, whose air is song,
Does he the Buddha of the West, belong?
He seems a winged Franklin, sweetly wise,
Born to unlock the secrets of the skies."[(2)]

Although the Transcendentalist circle was small, many acknowledged debts of gratitude to Emerson without necessarily adhering to his philosophy. In essence, the Transcendentalists were a first expression of an independent spiritual movement centered on the renewal of thinking and the re-awakening of a new intuition. It was a first successful step on the way towards bridging the mind and the heart.

Chapter 5

Thanksgiving, Pocahontas and the Dream of Brotherhood

"Then, joined the voice of first and least
A hymn of thanks we raise
Our day of fasting changed to feast
And prayer give way to praise"
(The First Thanksgiving, Boston 1631, Arhtur Guiterman)

In the present review of the festival we will direct our attention to the history of the beginnings of the first two colonies in Virginia and Massachusetts. The first two settlements on American ground have many more similarities than hitherto pointed out in historic literature. These emerge when we look in particular to the kind of relationships established between Native Americans and colonists. That new historical possibilities existed and were only partially actualized is what the American soul has come to intuit over the centuries. What is less known is the fact that the two colonies are intimately united by links of destiny.

Before looking at the Thanksgiving event, we will retrace the process that led to Thanksgiving being accepted as a national holiday. The process itself is very revealing about the nature of the holiday.

The Birth of the Holiday (1)

Thanksgiving is the holiday of family intimacy, a celebration of home and hearth. In this sense it contrasts strongly with the Fourth of July. Thanksgiving calls on the warmth of relationships rather than the light of great ideals. It is the celebration of the return to our origins: familial, cultural and religious. That such a simple, unpretentious festival had to struggle the longest in order to become an American holiday says much about its nature, although its intimate character would have us think otherwise.

The date of the first Thanksgiving is contested. Folklore has it celebrated first in the autumn of 1621, in Plymouth, Massachusetts. Virginians claim an earlier one on April 29th, 1607, the first officially held on Virginian soil by the Jamestown colony. Regardless of these particulars, that Thanksgiving is a characteristically New England festival cannot be denied. It evolved primarily in the towns of the Connecticut River and of the Plymouth colony. It was first proclaimed a state holiday in Connecticut in 1639. It became a regular celebration there from the year 1649 onwards, and was held every year thereafter in autumn. The celebrations included four hours of morning services and a home meal followed by another two hours of service. Thursday was chosen because it was the day devoted to lectures.

By the dawn of the 1700's the celebration spread to Massacchussets and New Hampshire, and the feast became as important as the morning service. There was no longer an afternoon service. During the Revolution Thanksgiving gradually became politicized. The day was often used as the occasion for the clergy to support the Revolution. The first national political Thanksgiving occurred on December 18th, 1777, in honor of Arnold's and Gates' victory at Saratoga. Samuel Adams had a part on the writing committee. There were celebrations each following year, except one, until 1784, which was celebrated as a Thanksgiving for peace.

Other political Thanksgivings fell in line. Washington issued one in 1789 for the blessing of the new form of government. He proclaimed only one other in 1795. On this occasion he was very careful to include " ...all religious denominations... and all persons". There was no reference to Christianity in his message. From this point onwards the holiday had to achieve Washington's goal and satisfy any and every religious / political outlook.

The issue of separation between Church and State and the rift between federalists and democratic republicans complicated the issues around the holiday. Precisely because of Jefferson's strict adherence to the separation of Church and State, Thanksgiving was eclipsed from his presidency. Nevertheless, with the expansion of the country, Thanksgiving traveled west with the New Englanders. In some states it was adopted even before the new territory had become an official state.

Another fault-line appeared at the time of the Civil War. The religious denominations were splitting along North-South and pro-slavery versus anti-slavery lines. Thanksgiving incorporated these debates. The holiday was called twice by Lincoln: first in 1863, then the following year when it became a national holiday. Official proclamations notwithstanding, many of the Southern states still resented the adoption of the festival accompanied with the victory of the Union. It was often either skipped or used to celebrate victories for the white supremacy rule.

We can see that it took more than two centuries for Thanksgiving to become a national celebration. Even after that, the holiday could not quite become a reality until all factional wounds were healed to a degree.

Thanksgiving is barely more than a hundred years old. It is a composite holiday borrowing from many sources. Its origins weld together at least four known holidays: the English Harvest Home, the political and religious Thanksgiving proclamations, and traces of Christmas.

Christmas enters here by way of exclusion. The Puritans disliked Catholic celebrations and had banned this major holiday. It reappeared nevertheless in the longing for the festive meal and mood. Harvest Home is a holiday of pagan origins, a festival of the harvest, accompanied with merriment and a proclivity to licentious behavior. Thanksgiving services already existed as such before the modern version arrived, both for marking political occasions declared by civil authorities and religious commemorations called for by clergymen or congregations.

From its historical origins, Thanksgiving can be seen as a hybrid holiday, another sort of Saint Tammany, almost a bundle of contradictions. Still, a look at a typical Thanksgiving a century and a half ago will show how all the different elements formed a whole, if not fully coherent, at least pointing towards a certain direction.

The services opened with the governor's Thanksgiving proclamation. The service included hymns, a Thanksgiving prayer that may last an hour or more and a sermon of up to two hours. A four-hour service was not considered unreasonable. The feasting, which followed after the service, had been the object of meticulous planning weeks ahead of time. The meats, stuffing, squashes, chicken pie and other sweet pies together with the plum pudding required careful preparation. The table displayed all the best that the farm or household could offer throughout the year. The meal would not begin until a long grace was said. This was an occasion for reviewing the blessings that the year had brought and asking for further blessings for the year to come.

The cornucopia, representing plenitude, is a fitting image for the Thanksgiving table. The turkey - the bird that looked so big and stood as a symbol of American abundance - seemed the perfect focus of a feast celebrating bountiful life. While family and friends appreciated the riches offered by the earth, the feasting also offered the occasion to review the year, not just in a material fashion but also in a reverential, grateful mood. Thanksgiving offered a time to look at all the foundations of the person's life: natural-geographic, ethnic and cultural, religious and spiritual. Upon all of these the personality is built.

As Thanksgiving became a national holiday it incorporated the remembrance of the nation's humble origins in the early seventeenth century. The romantic return to the first Thanksgiving is a recent addition, introduced during the middle and end of the 19th century. It depicts an image of idealized earthly contentment that results from the meeting of minds between Native American and European cultures. What had been true only in a very limited degree acquired the force of a leading cultural image.

As we can see from this image, Thanksgiving is a festival of inclusion, of embrace. To become such it had to make concessions and adjustments. Having been initially a Protestant holiday, Catholics viewed it with suspicion. It was only in 1884 that it was adopted by the Plenary Council of Catholic Bishops in Baltimore. It was during that time that Thanksgiving began to be celebrated with Union Services of inter-denominational character. At that time, immigration from Eastern and Southern Europe was viewed by many with alarm, as a threat against the American stock or tradition. Thanksgiving was put forth as a means of assimilation. The choice was fitting. To immigrants weary of changes and afraid of leaving behind their ethnic and religious background, the new holiday was welcoming, because it left them free to celebrate their own roots, with their own religious perspective and cultural choice of food, with the exception of the ubiquitous turkey. It offered them a foretaste of the American culture and a sense of assimilation.

A host of new habits accompanied the holiday. Thanksgiving became a day of sharing. It was considered a duty or honor to invite those who could not join their own families. These included foreigners or the underprivileged. It was and partly still is a habit to give a fitting Thanksgiving meal to the poor, to inmates, orphans or the sick. On this day, governors often offer pardons to prisoners.

Thanksgiving celebrates our ordinary ancestors. Likewise it was a seemingly ordinary woman who spread the conviction that the holiday should become a national celebration. Born in New Hampshire in 1788, Sarah Josepha Hale became a widow with five children. She decided to support her family with her literary gifts and wrote a rather controversial book which focused on the contrasts between the North and the South. It was called Northwood, or Life North and South. On the wake of her success, she accepted a job as editor of Ladies Magazine, one of the first women's magazines. Through this publication and her undeterred canvassing, she campaigned for a national Thanksgiving since the year 1846.

On the verge of the Civil War she appealed to people's reverence for Thanksgiving as a way to cement the Union, saying: "If every State should join in union Thanksgiving on the 24th of this month (November), would it not be a renewed pledge of love and loyalty to the Constitution of the United States, which guarantees peace, prosperity, progress, and perpetuity to our Republic." She wrote to Lincoln on this matter, two months before his second Thanksgiving proclamation.

In the light of the celebration of their national roots, the first two colonies - Plymouth and Jamestown - stand on equal footing. In the higher sense, no single colony could claim to be the better, just as no new immigrant is less valuable than the previous ones. Historically, the initial colonies of Virginia and Massachusetts share much more than appears on the surface. Both South Virginia (London Co.) and

North Virginia (Plymouth Co.), responsible for the establishment of the two colonies, were issued a charter in the spring of 1606. They were to respond to the Royal Council of Virginia, and subscribed to similar commercial and financial interests. The centralized form of government that derived from the Companies' prescriptions preserved little of the cherished freedoms of the Englishmen. Many of the first settlers in the two colonies were indentured servants. This state of servitude was not always a choice to which they had subscribed. (2)

In both colonies we find ordinary and extraordinary historical figures. As we shall see, one of them has by now become a legend.

First Americans: Links of Destiny

In the last fifty years there has been a growing desire to pierce through the veil of the 'First Thanksgiving' and give this image some flesh and blood. It has resulted in a series of popular books, mostly for children, around the figure of the Native American Squanto. Among those we can mention: Squanto and the First Thanksgiving, and Squanto, Friend of the Pilgrims. (3) Squanto's life is an astounding epic of unusual dimension for a Native American of the 17th century. By focusing on a quite uncanny and cosmopolitan biography the authors want to portray brotherhood in a more concrete manner. It is as if they pointed to the amount of overcoming that was necessary in order to bring closer both natives and pilgrims.

When we look at it with utmost self-honesty, we can realize that true brotherhood is still an ideal that we are mostly unable to live up to. We all wish it but intuit how far we are from it. This was all the more true in the 17th century. The colonists came as Christians who regarded the natives as cruel, barbarous and immoral. The gentleman would rather remain idle than join hands with the commoner. Competence was deemed a matter of social class. The Puritans or Separatists regarded themselves as saints and everyone else as strangers. The natives themselves were at war with each other and used alliances with the newcomers to weaken their adversaries. Political and personal freedom was an ideal, not a reality. Until the year 1618 the powers of the governor in the Virginia colony were practically powers of life and death. No less than some twenty offenses were punishable by death, and torture was also practiced. Among the listed crimes were such things as: seeking shelter with the natives or accepting food from them, attempting to return to England, stealing food from the stores or daring to criticize authority. [4]

When we steep ourselves in the mood of the time, the achievements of the few individuals we will consider acquire their true stature. Across the two colonies destiny forged links stronger then is currently known. In an ordinary way, the forces that we have recognized at work in the holiday of the Fourth of July were already apparent here, but the colonial reality of British imperialism held the upper hand. Despite this, there appeared at different times individuals able to stand against the oppressive influences of environment, race and culture. History seems to suspend its iron laws through the strength of one or a few individuals. This is what we want to trace. Although many of the facts are well known, they will be at least briefly mentioned to highlight the degree of interconnection between the characters of this historic drama. We need only look at three individuals to highlight this web of special relationships.

Captain John Smith

At the end of his life, an embittered lonely man held the claim that Plymouth and Jamestown were his two children. [5] Although a commoner by birth, this man was one of the most well-traveled individual of the times. He had fought as a soldier and mercenary and first met glory in Eastern Europe and in Asia. This part of his biography is filled with gallant captures and escapes, difficult to document from any other than Smith's own autobiography. Following these international escapades, he had a part in the founding of the colony of Jamestown in 1607. In a way uncommon to the times he became the only commoner to be included in the Council of the colony. However, he could not assume his new task, having been charged with mutiny during the ocean journey.

Although the Virginian colony owed its initial survival to the cooperation between Smith and Pocahontas, the captain's stay in Jamestown was not long. He left after September 1609, having to take care of an accidental wound. In the years in Jamestown he had proved his expertise in dealing with the Native Americans, although often taking advantage of their naivete. He was practically the only leader who respected them and was able to refrain from senseless retaliations.

In 1611, in England, he had contacted Ferdinando Gorges, governor of Plymouth and head of the North Virginia Company. Three years later Smith sailed to America with an Indian, by the same of Squanto, of whom more will be said later. (6) Smith may have known Squanto during his nine years of captivity in England. At any rate, the Native American was invaluable as an interpreter for trade dealings.

During the short trip, Smith undertook on his own initiative to map the East Coast from Maine to Massachusetts. He was the one who gave their present names to Patuxet and Accomac (later Plymouth). The region that he explored he called New England, a name later confirmed by Prince Charles. (7) Smith had other plans in mind. He hoped to establish a new colony and Plymouth was the place of his choice. In the year 1615, he was ready to give shape to his plans, but his preparations had obviously been hasty. Captain Dermer, second in command, rapidly vanished with one of the boats. Smith's ship was damaged in a storm and he had to return to Plymouth. He set out again, only to be attacked by pirates. The escapade made for an adventure matching his reputation.

In 1617, another of his hurried plans saw him sailing for America with only three ships out of thirty that had been promised to him. For three months he had been ready to leave, but the weather stood against him and he hesitated. Not far away, Pocahontas – who played an important part in his life - died at Gravesend from a pulmonary disease in March of that year.

In 1620, if not already in 1619, Smith had made contact with the Pilgrims in order to lead them to America. They were reluctant to take on a man who could not stoop to any role but that of a leader. The famous Standish was hired instead. Yet Smith still played a role. It was his maps that the Pilgrims took with them to the New World. (8) By another twist of fate, or possibly some hidden intention, the settlers landed in Plymouth rather than their initial destination at the mouth of the Hudson River. One cannot help but wonder if that happened by pure coincidence. After all Plymouth had been indicated by Smith as a good site for colonization. (9) Thus they reached the land to which Squanto had returned less than a year before.

Smith's life shows in a compelling way the network of relationships involved in the founding of the first two colonies. He is the tragic embodiment of a life failing to bring about any of its intended fruition, whether at Jamestown or Plymouth. The captain formed personal relationships with the two individuals whose lives shine as radiant symbols in the evolution of the two colonies: Squanto and Pocahontas.

Squanto (10)

For a time it was believed that there were two individuals with the name of Squanto (sometimes written Squantum or Tisquantum). This seemed the best way to explain how his name kept reappearing from one side of the ocean to the other. It has taken some time for historical research to put the pieces together and figure out that the name corresponds to just one individual.

Squanto belonged to the Patuxet, an Algonquian tribe of Massachussets, residing in the area of present day Plymouth. He was born between the years 1575 and 1780. His name first appears from the records of the expedition of Captain George Weymouth. He had been captured with four other Abnakis from the coast of Maine. This leads some to believe that he may have been on a journey to the Maine Algonquian tribe. In England he lived with Sir Ferdinando Gorges of the Plymouth Company. He is described by Gorges in his three-volume memoirs.

Squanto remained in England for nine years, before having the opportunity to return home with the expedition led by Captain Smith. It was a return for both of them. At the end of the journey he was released at Cape Cod and from there made it back to his tribe in Patuxet.

Thanks in large part to Smith's tolerant views, a conciliatory mood between the colonists and the native Indians had been established. In gratitude, the Patuxet held a celebration. Captain Hunt, Smith's second in command, took advantage of the Patuxet's relaxed attention to invite twenty-four of them aboard his ship. Once there, he made them captives and brought them to Spain to sell them as slaves.

To Squanto fell the relatively privileged position of being a slave to a monk. How he made it back to England has not been documented. He found refuge there with John Slanie who was the treasurer and later the president of the Newfoundland Company (also called the Bristol Company). [11] Aboard one of his ships Squanto made it back to the American continent in 1618, but only to Newfoundland. He was probably working for the fishing industry. The next year he sailed back home with Captain Thomas Dermer who worked for the Plymouth Company.

The homecoming was the harshest trial for Squanto. He discovered that his tribe had been entirely wiped out by the plague, most likely an outburst of chicken pox or measles. Thirteen years of exile and the loss of all his bloodline were the fruits of his contact with the white race. Soon after his return the familiar pattern of deceptions and reprisals was to play yet another role in Squanto's life. This time it was to come through Captain Dermer who had worked with Smith. After a senseless massacre committed by an English trader, the natives of the Wampanoag confederation intended to retaliate by killing Dermer who was there for trade. Squanto saved his life.

Without a people, and having raised suspicion of the neighboring tribes for his defense of a white man, Squanto returned with Dermer to Plymouth where he witnessed the arrival of the Pilgrims. He was introduced to them two months later by Samoset, a Sachem of the Abnaki of Maine, with whom Squanto had most likely been acquainted prior to his first abduction. There he joined the settlement permanently. Squanto's vital role in the colony has been abundantly acknowledged. He helped the settlers to grow crops and to fish for their sustenance. As an interpreter he helped to bring about the successful peace treaty that the Pilgrims drafted and eventually signed with the natives. More importantly, he helped to assure trade with the neighboring tribes.

Squanto's last years were marred by a climate of suspicion and distrust. Massasoit, the Wampanoag Sachem, had sent an ambassador to the pilgrims in the person of Hobomok. Rivalry developed between the two Indians and the Pilgrims took sides, partly in order to obtain major gains for themselves. Squanto attempted to strengthen his position by gaining power among the Wampanoag. To that end he used the native's superstitious fears of English weapons and diseases, and their belief that he had English support. Once discovered, only the Pilgrims could save him from Massasoit's death decree. This they did in memory of all the help they had received from him. Squanto died of an illness in 1622, while on a trading expedition with Governor Bradford. It appears that he converted to the Pilgrim's faith before his death.

Squanto carried further the process of rising above blood ties that Smith had initiated with Pocahontas. His destiny placed him in an even more dramatic position. He was well on the way to forming a bridge between the two cultures. Only later did he resort to cunning, succumbing to the prevailing atmosphere of distrust and deception.

Among the lesser participants of the founding drama of America, we have heard Dermer's name appear twice, first in relation to Smith, than associated with Squanto. His life course is shaped by the forces at play, while he seems to stand at the mercy of external factors that play alternatively in his favor and against him. He was supposed to be part of the intended Plymouth colony in 1615. When he returned there in 1619 Squanto saved him from Massasoit's vengeance. In the same year he traveled to Martha's Vineyard in order to trade. There he met with Epanow, Sachem of the natives, who at one point had also been a captive of the English. Epanow, afraid that Dermer might be there to capture him, killed all his party and left him with wounds that probably caused his death a year later in Virginia.

Pocahontas [12]

Pocahontas has achieved a level of literary and historical mystique. She has been called the Indian Princess, La Belle Sauvage, the Forest Princess, Virginia Sanpareil, the Female American, the Gentle Savage and many more epithets. In her lifetime she went by Pocahontas, more properly Matoaka and finally Lady Rebecca. Pocahontas was in fact a nickname by which she was known outside of the tribe. It meant 'playful, mischievous, frolicsome'. Her real name, Matoaka, was a secret name known only by the closest members of her clan but not used in everyday life.

A vast sequence of books has been written on her account over the last century and a half, and the flow hasn't dried up. The historical records cover only the last ten years of her life, from 1607 to 1617, and she even disappears for four of these (1609 to 1613). That such a fleeting historical presence should cause her to become a legend is enough to prove the depth of her impact on the American (and European) mind.

In her short life, the Powhatan princess gives proof of independence of mind together with sound judgement, strength to carry her resolves, compassion and adaptability. Being the favorite daughter of Powhatan - the chief of an Indian confederacy - gave her a status and respect with natives and Englishmen alike, that neither Squanto nor Smith could attain.

In the well-known first reported episodes of her life, she was the one who became acquainted with Captain Smith and taught him the rudiments of her Algonquian language. In the winter of 1607-08, when Smith was captured by Powhatan, Pocahontas interceded for his life. Whether it was a real rescue or a mock execution, the ordeal strengthened Smith's ties with the confederacy.

The colonists were plagued by the continuously fluctuating relationships with the natives as well as by their own inertia and bitter rivalries. During the first two winters it was Pocahontas who assured the survival of the settlers. She seemed to already act independently of her father, who was still undecided about what policy to follow with the foreigners. Pocahontas also had a restraining effect on Smith; on her behalf he released Indian prisoners in June of 1608.

The events accelerated dramatically at the end of 1608. Powhatan banned trade with the colonists and moved far from them to Werowocomoco, his capital. Powhatan actually planned to kill Smith, who had come on a trading mission. It was Pocahontas who saved him by unveiling her father's intentions, showing that she was taking further distance from Powhatan's policies. Displaying a complete lack of sensitivity, Smith wanted to reward her with trinkets.

Smith was later relieved of his power and ended up accidentally wounded in an attempt to form a separate colony. This is when he left the colony and Pocahontas was told that he had died. His departure left Pocahontas the diplomat without any intermediary. A cycle of senseless cruelty from the colonists and retaliations from Powhatan set in. In 1609 Powhatan ordered the massacre of sixty settlers.

Pocahontas removed to the farthest reaches of the confederacy, to the Patawomekes, a tribe that enjoyed a degree of autonomy from Powhatan. It was a first sacrifice on her part. She relinquished her status of privilege. Probably due to her influence the Patawomekes were the only ones who kept trading with the whites. Pocahontas also had a hand in saving Henry Spelman, a hostage who had escaped from the Powhatan, and was threatened with death from his ex-captives.

It is in the least expected way that Pocahontas played the role of mediator she seemed to be yearning for. In 1613 she was abducted in a colonists' ship. This episode was followed by her conversion to Christianity and her marriage to John Rolfe, a recently arrived settler. Pocahontas had to sacrifice the freedom of her ways in order to adapt to a rigid code of ethics. Yet she did it willingly. From this simple step emerged what was called the 'peace of Pocahontas' and dubbed a 'honeymoon between the races.' In effect Pocahontas brought her relatives and servants to live with her, inaugurating a level of cohabitation between the races unknown until that time. In the wake of these events, greater tolerance prevailed between colonists and natives.

In the spring of 1616, Pocahontas went to England. Behind the stated purpose of promoting a Christian school for English and native children was the more substantial, promotional aspect that the Virginia Company needed. At the time it was still struggling to remain afloat and encourage new colonists. Pocahontas suffered from various challenges. It was in England that Pocahontas met again with John Smith, whom she still believed dead. We can only surmise the impact of the encounter, and whether this was another contributing factor on top of the cultural shock and the poor sanitation of London that led her to contract what seems to have been a respiratory disease. She died of it on March of 1617.

Destiny and Brotherhood

In the drama of the foundation of the new nation a host of actors play important roles. By looking at three of them, whose lives we have just examined, we can touch upon most of the central issues and uncover significant relationships. The lives of these three individuals highlight how one's use of freedom of choice leads to different outcomes. We can marvel at how the lives of these individuals keep intersecting in a way that has very little to do with mathematical probability or random chance. It would seem pure speculation to wonder at the effects of courageous individual decisions or to envision scenarios that didn't occur. We will see that this is not an idle exercise. Destiny is not an inescapable, preset path. It leaves many choices and often offers many more than one opportunity in order to achieve certain goals.

In the society of the seventeenth century Smith's natural capacities, standing and authority were of no avail against social prejudices. His relentless assertiveness and complete lack of tact were his downfall. They also played against him in the Pilgrim's mind; Miles Standish was chosen as leader instead.

The vacuum created by Smith's absence required all the more energy and willingness on the part of Pocahontas. It remains pure speculation to contemplate what Plymouth could have been with the help of both Smith and Squanto, who already knew each other. Ironically, it was in Standish that Squanto found a resolute adversary. The Native American faced a different temptation than Smith did. Not having the charisma and sheer bravado of the captain, Squanto resorted to cunning and deceit in order to circumvent the distrust of both natives and settlers.

In Pocahontas a process was brought to completion. She had the strengths of both Smith and Squanto. In addition she could stand above the warring parties with firmness and compassion. By her unwillingness to accommodate or compromise and seek an outlet to her ambition, she managed to fulfill what seems to have been her life task. To accomplish this task she willingly paid the price imposed by the deceit of the colonists and of the Virginia Company. There was nothing artificial in her acceptance of Christianity. It came to her through Alexander Whitaker, a man who had left a life of ease to come to Virginia, and showed complete tolerance towards the natives. [13] Through him, John Rolfe was able to overcome his pangs of consciousness at the idea of marrying a 'savage' woman.

The contradictory future of the colony stood fittingly represented by the two-sided image of John Rolfe. His devotion and earnestness seemed genuine. Through him came both the 'Peace of Pocahontas' and the rescue of the Virginia Company's financial interests. It was Rolfe who successfully introduced the tobacco culture into the new colony, assuring it an economic outlet. Rolfe could not see the full implication of his experiments, other than the fact that they assured him a place in society well beyond his humble origins. He witnessed and recorded the arrival of the first cargo of African slaves brought by a Dutch boat in 1619 without registering the full impact of this precedent. His son, Thomas Rolfe, displayed great courage when, in 1641, he wanted to establish contacts with his Native American bloodline. This was at a time when the colonists had severed all relationships with the natives, following the massacre of three-hundred-forty-seven colonists in March of 1622. How he came to reverse his position is not known. By 1646 he was actively participating in the genocide of his people. He became in effect a lieutenant in the colonial militia.

Through Pocahontas' devoted life history escapes the momentarily unavoidable play that the stronger political and economic forces of the moment bring to the surface. A sort of island in space and time is created by the commitment of an individual fully living on the strength of her moral intuitions, even at the cost of repeated sacrifice.

In Pocahontas the ideal of brotherhood is strongly rooted. Although she stands within the forces of race, religion and culture as do her contemporaries, the vigor of her individuality can rise above them. Her moral feelings and principled positions would surely puzzle one who believes only in racial, social or environmental determinism.

Destiny is a mysterious concept for some, an intuited reality for others. The individual can either accept destiny passively, with a feeling of fatalism, or blindly rebel against it. There is also a third, intermediate possibility. We can call it 'active acceptance', but it could also be called 'active questioning'. Active acceptance is an attitude that questions the given social and environmental conditions of the times. It challenges them with a constructive attitude at the opposite pole of pure rebellion or strict conformity. It stems from the realization that our life has both a set of constraints that we can free ourselves from and another set of constraints that we need to learn to accept. We may be born with a physical, mental or developmental handicap. Accepting this element of our destiny is the recognition that even those constraints that we cannot free ourselves from are not arbitrary baggage imposed on us by a malevolent god. This may not lead us into altogether denying our human potential or railing against the limitations set by fate or by genes. This active acceptance derives from either having or developing a strong individuality. Helen Keller is a fitting example. It would be difficult to think of her life without her disability. That she offered humanity the gift of her warmth and compassion comes precisely from having to live with her challenges. These enabled her to offer solutions and alternatives for all those who suffered as she did.

Another implicit element of active acceptance is the capacity to forgive. Forgiving has even linguistic similarities with forgetting. Yet it is a conscious forgetting, quite the contrary from denying, which occurs in the unconscious. In order to forgive the individual must fully know the pain of the offense that has been inflicted upon her. She has to build the strength and desire to be able to give back to the world as much as has been taken away through the offending deed. Forgiveness is also the trust in the presence of spiritual powers of good who are able to guide the individual in order to reestablish the social balance that the offending deed has altered. The odyssey of Hiawatha serves as a clear illustration of the act of forgiveness. Hiawatha could forgive the death of his wife and daughters because the spiritual powers were showing him the reality of the message of Deganawidah. Hiawatha could hold that higher reality in front of his eyes. His faith was the very force that allowed that higher reality to also become earthly reality.

This strength of individuality that actively accepts destiny and offers forgiveness is recognizable in Pocahontas. Active acceptance is as much an affirmation of our own individuality as a submission to a spiritual world above us. Through such a free choice, healing can enter a community of individuals. Acceptance of our destiny, as we see from Pocahontas' life, is an act that needs to be renewed repeatedly. Through such active acceptance we can bring deeper resolve and determination to our activities in the world.

While unaccepted and undigested individual experiences act as a burden on the individual and as an anti-social force in the community, active acceptance of destiny and the forces of forgiveness that it generates act as a solvent that defuses social strife. Pocahontas' resolve for forgiveness brings about the ensuing years of peace. Throughout her life she strives to bring about the recognition of the universal spiritual element that unites communities beyond race, culture or religion. In this light her conversion experience is secondary. There is no marked difference between her behavior before or after it.

Seen without the elements of acceptance and forgiveness, Pocahontas' life becomes a legend. Her behavior escapes the deterministic paradigm that materialism embraces. Of all the actors on the scene of the founding colonies she is the least predictable because she is the most determined from within. It is in the ideal of brotherhood that Pocahontas becomes the first American heroine, as she has been fittingly named.

The future of America lay encapsulated in the contrast between Pocahontas and the Virginia Company. The Virginia Company ruled its territory like a business or a production unit. It was a symbol of the monopolies that exploited the colonies for the mother country. Monopolies rested on the alliance between the political system and the economy. Merchants would benefit from the exclusion of all competition; politicians would benefit from the company's fortunes. The Virginia Company would naturally have to be supported by the might of England's navy. The fate of an economic-financial pursuit thus came to be confused and assimilated with the interests of the English people at large.

In America the Virginia Company promoted the development of mono-culture. The fate of the southern colonies, as we have seen from our study of mercantilism, was a destiny of debt. The planters could not support themselves free of debt, even in spite of having access to the free labor of slaves. Slavery itself embodies the ultimate state of debt. The slave's life was not his to decide upon. He owed it to somebody else. The slaves' individualities were blotted out in order to make of them mere mechanisms in a production unit. The slave owners weren't the real beneficiaries of this state of debt, they were mainly intermediaries. The real beneficiaries of this human exploitation were the economic and political class, which supported the economic monopolies. They sacrificed to their own interests the destinies of those who carried forward their goals.

That Pocahontas is a polar opposite to this first image isn't as easy to see at first. The Indian princess ended her life at the hand of the greed of the Virginia Company that used her as a promotional tool. Before that, Pocahontas' generosity and open-mindedness unlocked new possibilities for others. Being the daughter of a king allowed her to extend help to Captain Smith. When she lost his and her father's support, she was still trading with the English through the Patawomekes and keeping a door open for peaceful cohabitation. Even her abduction opened new possibilities through her ensuing marriage. Through her agency other individuals were given back the ground wherein their human potential could fully develop. Pocahontas took upon herself acceptance accompanied by willed self-sacrifice. This was the sacrifice of personal ambition, desire for power over others, and other life-negating natural human urges. Through this sacrifice she did not renounce her own quest for happiness. It appears that she could find it as well as providing the ground for other people's happiness.

The Virginia Company took every step to limit people's freedoms when they stood in the way of its own pursuit of economic interest. It is no wonder that no true individuality stands among its ranks to be remembered to this day. Pocahontas offered the opposite. Her presence offered to others the chance to unfold their personality in a climate of peace that was conducive to self-development. To the sacrifice imposed on others by the Virginia Company, Pocahontas offered the complement of healthy self-sacrifice that opens new, creative paths in the social body. This image aptly resumes the contrast of world visions that stood visible at the foundation drama of America.

Looking at the larger picture, the 'peace of Pocahontas' was doomed so long as the colonists pursued the interests of the monopolies that stood behind them. There was no place in their plans for a cohabitation with the natives, far from it. In fact slavery was their next 'necessary' step. The basis for a deeper brotherhood lay much further on the horizon. Brotherhood seems in this respect like a seed that germinates, but keeps dying prematurely until a better or more adapted seed takes on and brings fruit.

We have characterized the process bringing forth a new form of government and of new social relationships within the context of the Fourth of July. This is a turning point of history, as much a new beginning as the culmination of past efforts. For an even partial defeat of the predicament of the economic policies of British Imperialism, new spiritual forces needed to gain strength. Washington and Franklin arrived at the culmination of events started by the lesser known and unaccounted heroes like Squanto and Pocahontas. The two founding fathers could play a larger role in history precisely because the ground had already been richly prepared.

We could analyze certain phenomena in this light. Was it mere chance that Philadelphia acted as the mid-wife to a process of innovation culminating in the new form of government? Was not Philadelphia already the center of what was called the Holy Experiment, a haven for persecuted people and ideas? There, the relationships between colonists and Native Americans, although not perfect, had at least another tenor; wars were avoided. Didn't such cultural ferment attract the brilliant mind of Franklin and allow the development of countless of his ideas? Didn't it later usher the early development of Freemasonry among other things? Didn't it allow Franklin to understand and appreciate the ideas of the Iroquois? In between these stages we could mention the role played by the Moravian missionaries in Pennsylvania, or the role played by Conrad Weiser - who had been raised by the Iroquois - as emissary of the colony to the Native Americans. The small turning points - like the Peace of Pocahontas - may be swallowed by the course of history and seemingly amount to little, but the social healing created by them is real and enduring. They provide the foundations for later, fundamental changes

Conclusion

After the American Dream: The Future of the Three Holidays

"…a third joyful anniversary is sealed for the American Republic:
The twenty second of February is sacred to the memory of Washington and patriotic duties.
The Fourth of July is the Jubilee of national independence.
The last Thursday in November, let it be consecrated to our Father in heaven.
For His bounteous blessing bestowed upon us, as the perpetual day of Thanksgiving of the American people."
(Sarah Hale in 1865, just after the adoption of a national Thanksgiving Day)

As Sarah Hale intuited, the three festivals can be seen as a whole. In fact we may say that they form a progression. What this generous woman of the 19th century interpreted in a religious-patriotic way can now be reinterpreted in order to encompass the modern spiritual strivings of the American people.

The three festivals have shown us which European and Native American cultural/spiritual influences were at work at the birth of the nation, even when to all appearances they did not unite, or did so in a very poor fashion. Sometimes such events happened in a popular spontaneous fashion. Tammany is a case in point. At other times inspired individuals carried in their hearts and minds the destinies of their communities or of the whole nation. Such were Pocahontas, Deganawidah, Franklin, Washington and others. Finally, there were repeated instances of extended cultural cross-pollination. The Iroquois' adoption of many colonists, for instance, played a considerable role to which history seldom gives its due.

Hidden America

We can now revisit the three holidays in light of the history of the founding of the nation. We can recall the intuition of Carl Stegmann about the American Dream:

> *"... what is meant if, as is frequently done, one speaks of the "American dream?" It is the feeling that something was at work at the founding of America that was "not of this world", something that arose out of primal creative dreams of the world, out of forces of the world, out of forces working unbeknown to human beings. A creative dream can rise up at any time in suitable individuals, and has indeed emerged in them."* (1)

We have tried to understand this dream and identify its dreamers. It seems that it was this quality of 'dream' that allowed America to preserve the forces of religion and spirituality, delaying for maybe another two centuries the process that had everywhere began to spread in Europe. Nowhere is the contrast more evident than between the American and the French Revolutions. The latter started very much from similar premises. Along the way, and due to the historic circumstances such as the role of the church and monarchy, the ideas of the revolution became completely secular and were severed from their spiritual sources. The permeation of social striving with the religious/spiritual is not a given in America either. As evolution progresses the old ideas cannot sustain us anymore. The American Dream that inspired the holidays we have observed is receding into the memory of the nation. All the forces that contributed to it have themselves exhausted their impetus. Therefore the holidays have lost much of their inner meaning, especially for the younger generations. As is only natural in the cycle of cultural renewal, new forces need to come to the fore. Some of these are already discernable that would allow us to revive the holidays and imbue them with new meaning. Each dream needs to be brought to the light of consciousness in order to become more than a dream.

With our first holiday we have remained in the realm of prehistory and myth. Although having vague roots in history, the Tammany of the colonists possessed mythic overtones. The Saint Tammany celebrations indicated the need for spiritual knowledge to flow into the culture of the times through the figure of the saint-king. Saint Tammany's stood for spiritual freedom. The symbol of the buck-tail and the Native American element point to the freedom of the wilderness. Liberty, as seen in the symbol of Tammany, derives from the civilizing hero who brings renewed spiritual impulses. Through these social peace is restored. The renewal of society is therefore completely tied into its spiritual health, and the vigor and independence of culture. Strife and decadence set in when the spiritual is forgotten.

More of the idea of spiritual freedom lived in an undefined Tammany than later survived in Washington. Any historical figure remains bound to the time in which he lived. By necessity Washington represents much less than the original Tamanend. His image also represents less for modern consciousness than it did two hundred years ago. Paradoxically, spiritual freedom is the element that is the most threatened and more urgently in need of renewal in American society. The cultural sphere is the most precarious area of social life. The renewal of the political and economic arenas greatly depends upon it.

Franklin and Emerson showed us the way into the realm of spiritual freedom. Modern Americans as well as modern man in general, need to find a way to the spirit that is not tied to dogma or sectarianism. It needs to be individual as well as universal. Franklin and Emerson, the two pioneers of American spirituality, show us that moral individualism is possible. This is an approach to the existential riddles of life that does not deny the modern scientific spirit. Rather it extends its methodology to all fields of knowledge. To do so something must be added to the dry, cold approach of science, that we usually recognize as being completely divested of morality - as it were 'morally neutral'. Franklin would have called the complement of this approach 'moral algebra', Emerson named it 'intuitive thinking'.

Throughout time, humanity has been guided by spiritual traditions and organized religion. Franklin, as well as Emerson, spent their lives wrestling with the 'inner question'. What religions and world traditions of East and West taught them was something they could approach with the open-mindedness of a true scientist, someone who does not need to take ideas on faith, and cannot reject what he has not tested. This was their contribution to American spirituality. Morality, the question that America often struggles with, needs to be redefined from within the shrine of the individual. No outer codes of ethics and behavior can give lasting satisfaction to the American mind any longer.

The new approach to spirituality will have to withstand the test of individual freedom as well as ethical individualism.

Many signs indicate that a first stage of this renewal has been achieved. More and more people in America are starting to look at all the decisions that affect their lives, trying to provide responses that originate from new cultural/spiritual perspectives. They are starting to shape an alternative paradigm to the economically driven culture of our times. Our passive consumption of television culture, the way we invest our money, the schools we send our children to, the food we eat and products we buy are all parts of the puzzle that we define as culture and that provides meaning to our lives. Making conscious choices that preserve the environment, respect human labor and truly inform the consumer or add beauty to our lives is their way to create a new culture and change reality before waiting for political change.

The press has spawned countless new ground-breaking publications. People who normally looked for answers solely within the political arena have started to realize that change occurs also through personal choices. More and more magazines tie together political issues with larger cultural perspectives. Themes of spirituality and choices of lifestyle are often discussed side by side with political themes and woven into the larger picture of social change. At bottom culture finds a place as equal next to politics.

Modern consciousness itself is manifesting changes that modify our way of perceiving life and its mysteries. The phenomenon of Near Death Experiences has touched a growing number of individuals, especially since the last half of the twentieth century. It cannot be given either a positive or a negative connotation in and of itself. What is a fact, however, is the possibility conferred on the individual of gaining new perspectives on the reality of the spiritual world. Ideas that flowed into our culture through faith or dogma can now be revisited at the level of experience and infuse society with new values. If spiritual reality is earnestly experienced within the shrine of the individual, society is bound to be transformed by it, no matter how little. The spiritual experience that deeply affected Bill Wilson in 1934 gave him the impetus for the founding of Alcoholics Anonymous five years later. We know what deep influence the Twelve-Step Programs have had ever since on our social environment.

Conclusion

The sociologist Paul Ray has indicated that a growing section of our population can be called 'cultural creative'. Basically this is a tendency towards the emancipation of culture from the driving tenets of political forces that too often closely identify or merge with the prevailing economic interests. The segment of population identified as 'cultural creative' is only slowly starting to gain an awareness of itself, and will gradually become able to represent more than a tendency or attitude towards life. It can in effect bring about a cultural renewal closely allied to spiritual renewal at the individual level. We can recognize that the cultural realm has started to claim an area of autonomy from the political realm. The recent term 'Civil Society' also underscores the need of holding for culture a space that is independent from politics or economy. Political activism lives alongside social activism and cultural activism, depending on how individuals envision their role in society. All of the terms are encompassed by another we are starting to hear - 'visionary'- a term pointing to spiritual experience.

In examining the significance of the Fourth of July we have moved from a myth into the world of history and legend. Legend in this case means a concrete historical event clothed in imaginative language. We have also seen how the moral strength of the crafts, that lived in the Templars, materialized in the building of the cathedrals and the molding of a new social reality. This very same influence reappeared, modified, later in time through the contribution of early Freemasonry.

The Iroquois contributed another important part to the process of developing the new form of government. Hiawatha is the quintessential new social hero. Modifying the existing social order requires a willingness to sacrifice old assumptions. Deganawidah, source of inspiration to others, can only freely give his ideas to groups of people willing to sacrifice their old point of view, willing to acquire the New Mind. The paradoxical figure of Atotarho is central to the legend. It is through him that the Five Nations can create the new strength necessary for their goals. Atotarho's healing is the culmination of the whole drama.

Social renewal is not the result of ideas alone. Ideas must be accompanied by deeds. Social change requires a universal vision. It calls on all of us to acknowledge that "all men are created equal". Hiawatha's desire to alleviate suffering became the ability to extend forgiveness. Social change will have to rest upon these and similar attitudes. The so-called 'evil' itself will have to be re-evaluated as a step towards a higher good. Deganawidah's and Hiawatha's most lasting inheritance is the knowledge that evil is only working against progress in the short term. The healed Atotarho can himself contribute to a new level of civilization that didn't exist before his active opposition.

The Fourth of July is a holiday completely rooted in the political realm. The American form of government is the first successful, albeit imperfect social architecture, deriving from the ideas of early Freemasonry. Enshrined within it is the constant concern for true equality under the law and, in an embryonic form, the separation and healthy inter-relation of the spheres of society: cultural, political and economic. Other, more elaborate social compacts can evolve from the first form that the American government has represented.

The Constitution' s value lay in the fact that it came about through a long process of education and 'active compromise'. Let us look closer at these two pre-requisites. The revolutionary war was for Washington, otherwise a mediocre general, the opportunity to teach his soldiers as well as the population of the colonies how the new ideas had to be fought for and promoted. It wasn't a matter of just winning. The means were so much more important than the end. The contrast with the French Revolution is enlightening in this regard. Inflammatory slogans, to all appearances justified, led first to violence, then to extended terror and finally to dictatorship. The American Revolution was a process giving its due to the voice of consciousness. Everyone could participate in it, even as an opponent. Active compromise was the effort of finding common ground, rather than clinging to pre-established goals. It was an effort to believe that truth lay somewhere in between all individual truths, and that no-one could claim to know the ultimate 'truth' at any given time. Active compromise is an act of faith wherein even the affairs of nations depend in no small measure upon the collaboration of the spirit. Such a message can be deeply meditated upon in all spheres of social life today. It has by no means been attained and generalized.

In this area, as in the cultural realm, new trends have emerged that can work as forces of healing in the social sphere. It has been more than sixty years since Alcoholics Anonymous came into being. Since then countless other movements have spawned from this basic idea. A. A. is rooted in an acknowledgement of the spiritual world, devoid of dogma and independent from any religious denomination or even religion itself. A cornerstone of the Twelve-Step Programs lies in the recognition that self-development is rooted in the strength of our inter-connectedness. We cannot grow and change except through others. This process can be raised to consciousness and be made use of deliberately in order to help our fellow man. The thousands of people who have internalized the skills and processes taught in these groups can act as agents for social change in every walk of life.

The spreading of crisis lines or hotlines forms a network of care and concern that implements social change in small doses. The ideas of a free spirituality and true equality between human beings are the sine qua non of the twelve-step groups, crisis lines and countless other support or peer groups. These are small seeds that can gradually help to transform the landscape of human relations that lie at the basis of the political process.

It is becoming more and more obvious that social transformation will develop from the ability to listen, exert tolerance towards others and rid oneself of destructive habits. The 'think locally/act globally' perspective shows us that social/political problems are also the reflection of challenges that live at the smallest levels of society. At bottom lies the ability to rethink politics beyond the limiting tenets of a basic dualism. The present paradigm clings to the belief that every wrong idea or inefficient governance can be solved through opposition and the replacement of the governing party with the opposing party. It is in effect a view that often perpetuates the evil it is supposed to fight. The legend of the White Roots of Peace has shown us that we need to think beyond dualism. Such an understanding is manifested in the idea of coalitions. The old socio-political boundaries are starting to melt in front of the ability to truly meet one another. Traditional adversaries are finding new ways to work together and expanding their goals. Workers are starting to meet with environmentalists that they usually saw at odds with their interests. Similar alliances are frequently built between different races and even across political divides.

The ills that we are supposed to fight have to be transformed, not suppressed. The movements of social renewal that we have enumerated are helping us to gain consciousness of the fact that we have all been part of the problem and part of the solution at different times in our lives. Social renewal comes from the transformation of the evil that lives in society and is potentially present in every human being, much more so than from a simple suppression of an objective outer evil.

Finally, in Thanksgiving something new appeared. We moved into the sphere of biography and relationships, the purely personal, in order to recognize links of destiny. This is also the area of economic relationships. What is it that unites Native Americans and European settlers in an encounter that could otherwise be a caprice of chance? Thanksgiving is one of the rare holidays, if not the only one, where a nation acknowledges the divine principle outside of any consideration of dogma or organized religion.

Thanksgiving invites us to recognize that, given our divine origin, not only are we equal, as the Declaration of Independence states, but also brothers. Thanksgiving gives new meaning to the idea of brotherhood. The evolving image of the celebration invites us to seek brotherhood at a deeper level than existed in nineteenth century Romanticism. The idea of destiny and the opportunities that it offers to individuals will in time give us tools for a deeper understanding of the events that we recognize in the founding of the nation.

At present there are many hindrances in the social realm which prevent recognition of true individuality that goes hand in hand with an idea of destiny that Emerson described and Pocahontas embodied. The vast problem of race is also one of the clearest challenges facing America. Nowhere else in the world do all races intermingle as they do in this country. Every continent is represented in America's racial fabric. The nation came to birth in Philadelphia, city of 'brotherly love', already the meeting place of many different cultures. The problem of race is intimately intertwined with economic reality and needs to be approached primarily from this angle. The appalling economic inequalities constitute true barriers to the perception of our brothers of other races. However, racism cannot be overcome as long as the individual is looked at only from purely deterministic perspectives. When that which is universal is perceived in the individual, he will be accepted for his innate value and not solely defined as the product of environment, race or religion. By the same token, prejudices will tend to dissolve the more we understand and perceive our culture, race and religion, or all our personal traits and preferences as the outer garment and not the deepest essence of our being. The outer sheath has to be fully given its credit. Later we can realize that it represents only a part of the human being. Fully acknowledging the reality of outer and inner worlds could be the beginning of a true brotherhood.

Growing to understand our destiny and realizing that it is completely woven with the social fabric and the destiny of others is a step towards true brotherhood. This view is present whenever we learn to take responsibility for everything around us and acknowledge that we have power to create and modify our environment. Countless initiatives show it every day. Community service and other forms of volunteerism are some of the driving forces of America and a response that surges in times of need or crisis. Organizations like Care International, Oxfam, Amnesty International, Save the Children, and quite a few others presently have yearly budgets of above $100 million. It is not possible to circumscribe these international organizations to national boundaries. A considerable part of their strength nevertheless derives from the United States.

America has repeatedly brought forth new utopias and new lifestyles. In the 19th century it gave birth to a great number of utopian communities. The dream resurfaced in the sixties, and many say that it was the victim of its own naivete. However, the willingness to experiment drives these partial and unsuccessful forerunners towards the greater level of awareness that makes new experiments grow mature. Organic and community supported agriculture, Fair Trade products, socially responsible investing, the development of land trusts, co-housing initiatives, or spiritual communities devoted to service are modeling and pioneering new forms of earth stewardship and social relationships.

Let us look at a single one of these initiatives: the Hospice Movement. The hospices that existed in the Middle Ages had a wider set of functions than the present idea. Mostly centered around monasteries they weren't necessarily limited to the care of the dying. The idea survived later on mainly through religious institutions. In this country modern hospices were introduced in the seventies. These institutions look at the dying patient from an interdisciplinary approach that includes medical, psychological and spiritual elements; they do this through the help of professionals and volunteers. The hospices' goal is to give back human dignity to those who die. In true hospice work, according to many witnesses, boundaries become tenuous between work and service done in love without care for the clock. Professionals, volunteers and patients feel in effect part of a community of common concern. Care of the dying allows families to experience peace at critical turning points. In this way hospices act as powerful agents for community healing by restoring those bonds that the modern care of the dying has severed. They are in effect agents for social change as much as professional institutions. They actively embrace and embody new ways to bring about the idea of brotherhood.

There were only three full-fledged hospices in 1975. The growth of the movement in the last three decades has profoundly impacted American society. It isn't however their numbers, still limited, as the quality of their community building that has brought about a new set of values in the fabric of society. Death was still a taboo topic in the seventies. Habits have changed. Dying is more easily talked about, classes are offered in colleges, and books and resources are more easily available. A revolution has gone full circle. What was once just a small practical initiative in the economic realm, has injected new values into our culture.

An overall view of the three holidays allows us to distinguish the tendencies of America's past, present and future. Saint Tammany celebrated in a pre-conscious fashion the American soul's desire for deeper spiritual sources of inspiration. It looked back to a distant past in order to inspire the present. Modern spirituality requires that we now seek a conscious knowledge of the spiritual world.

The Fourth of July is the holiday most connected with the present. It is the one addressing the social realm. What came as fruition and end-product of 18th century Freemasonry and Iroquois spirituality left us a seed that can now evolve further. The process the nation underwent two centuries ago remains an example whose essence can be successfully emulated in social processes at all levels. New social forms can only improve the imperfect ones of the past on the basis of a clear understanding of the laws affecting human relationships and social processes.

Finally, Thanksgiving - the most recent of the three holidays - has a more prophetic nature. When we celebrate our common Father in the heavens, we implicitly recognize that we are all brothers, regardless of race, religion and all outer appearances. Thanksgiving helps us to build an image of the brotherhood that can be attained in the future. We will then need to awaken to that 'sense for destiny' that Emerson felt and eloquently described. This is what will enable us to look at the world as Pocahontas did, and learn to see the universally human qualities in our fellow human being. It is fitting that Pocahontas has been called 'the first American', indicating perhaps the future direction of America's unfolding mission.

REFERENCES AND NOTES

Chapter 1: The Role of Religion in the 18th Century

1) *Under the Cope of Heaven: Religion, Society, and Politics in Colonial America*, Patricia U. Bonomi, 1986, Oxford University Press, pp. 4 and 220.

2) Ibid., p. 195.

Chapter 2: From Saint Tammany to Washington's Day: Evolution of a Holiday

1) *Official History of the Improved Order of Red Men*, Charles C. Conley, George W.Lindsay, Charles H. Litchman, 1893, The Fraternity Publishing Co., Boston, pp. 158-159.

2) The Wallam Olum is the oldest recorded document of Native North American history. After the arrival of the whites, a party of Lenni Lenape was retreating from Pennsylvania. to Ohio and Indiana. In one village a deadly epidemic struck the family of an Olumpee, a record keeper. A certain doctor Ward succeeded in curing the patient and in exchange he received the wooden records of the Wallam Olum. Unable to decode them, the doctor gave them to the botanist, archaeologist, scientist and linguist, Constantine Samuel Rafinesque, in 1820. In 1822, Rafinesque obtained from another individual the lyrics that accompanied the symbols of the Wallam Olum but he couldn't understand or translate the language. He had access to the Moravian archives of Bethlehem which had dictionaries and word lists of Delaware (Lenni Lenape) language. By acquiring the sung verses, Rafinesque was able to decode the pictographs. The symbols contain several combined ideas in compound ideograms. Rafinesque was able to translate the document in 1833. In 1836 he published *The American Nations, or Outlines of Their General History, Ancient and Modern*, containing the translation of the Wallam Olum without the symbols. The original pictographs have since been lost. Fortunately Lenni Lenape traditions were recorded in the early years of British colo-

nization, and anthropology as well as archaeology have contributed to the solving of the puzzle.
From: *The Red Record, the Wallam Olum: the Oldest Native North American History*, David Mc Cutchen, 1989, Avery Publishing Group, Garden City Park, New York.

3) See: *The Red Record, the Wallam Olum: the Oldest Native North American History*, opus quoted, pp. 99-100 for Tamanend I, and pp. 130, 150 for Tamanend II.

4) *Saint Tammany and the Origin of the Society of Tammany or Columbian order in the City of New York*, Edwin, P. Kilroe, 1913, M. B. Brown, New York, p. 29.

5) *America B. C.: Ancient Settlers in the New World*, Barry Fell, 1976, Pocket Books, New York, p. 44, and
Explorations in America Before Columbus, Hjalmar Holand, 1958, Twayne Publishers, New York, pp. 154-160.

6) *America B. C.: Ancient Settlers in the New World*, opus quoted, pp. 45 and 61.

7) *The Search for Lost America*, Salvatore M. Trento, 1978, Contemporary Books Inc., Chicago, p. 158.

8) *America B. C.*, opus quoted, p. 206.

9) *Bronze Age America*, Barry Fell, 1982, Little, Brown and Company, pp. 96,101,165, 217-220, 228, etc.

10) Ibid.

11) *The Search for Lost America*, opus quoted, pp. 120, 181.

12) *America B. C.*, opus quoted, pp. 96, 127-128.

13) *Bronze Age America*, opus quoted, pp. 173-174, 227, 230-235.

14) *Ancient Celtic America,* William R. Mc Glone, Phillip M. Leonard, 1986, Panorama West Books, Fresno, CA.

15) *Bronze Age America,* opus quoted, pp. 158-159, 191-192.

16) *America B. C.,* opus quoted, pp. 200, 209-210, 213.

17) *The Ancient Splendor of Prehistoric Cahokia,* Sidney Denny, Ernest L. Schusky 1992, Arressico Publ., Edwardsville, Illinois, pp. 44-5.
See also:
Cahokia Woodhenge update, Warremn L. Wittry, in *Archaeoastronomy Journal,* Vol. 3 of Winter 1980.
and
The American Woodhenge, Warren L. Wittry, in *The News Letter,* Cranbrook Institute of Science, Vol 33, # 9, Bloomfield Hills, Michigan, pp. 102-107.

18) *Formalhaut and Cairn D at the Big Horn and Moose Mountain Medicine Wheels,* Jack H. Robinson. See also:
Vision Quest at the Big Horn Medicine Wheel and its Date of Construction, Allan G. Fries, in *Archaeoastronomy Journal,* vol. 4 of Nov.-Dec. 1980.

19) *The Sacred Pipe: Black Elk's Account of the Seven Rites of the Oglala Sioux,* Joseph Epes Brown, 1953, University of Oklahoma Press.

20) *Saint Tammany and the Origin of the Society of Tammany or Columbian order in the City of New York,* opus quoted, pp. 32, 38-39, 94.

21) *The Life, Exploits and Precepts of Tammany, the Famous Indian Chief,* S. L. Mitchill, oration delivered at Old Presbyterian Church, New York, on May 12, 1795, microfilm.

22) *Official History of the Improved Order of Red Men,* opus quoted, see Chapter 4: Society of Red Men (1813-1833)
From this document we have insight into the importance of ritual and the blending of typical Masonic ceremonies with Native American overtones. The applicants had to be proposed by a

'brother'. A committee would then inquire into the candidate's fitness and character. Acceptance had to be subscribed by a unanimous vote. Later the neophyte would be placed under the tutelage of the Door Keeper who offered him instruction and presented him to the Generalissimo. The 'would-be-member' was questioned regarding his citizenship, his motives for seeking to join, and warned that "Red Men are men without fear, and that none but such could be grafted into the tribe."

Once again the neophyte would be presented to the Generalissimo for further instructions. Part of these read: "Red Men administer no oaths binding you to any political or religious creed...The motto of the society is 'freedom', and while claiming its privileges and blessings for ourselves, we aim no less to exert toleration to others." This was followed by a request for trustworthiness and faithfulness to their ideals. Additionally the neophyte had to keep the rituals secret from the uninitiated. After adoption, the society conferred on the new member a hierarchical title and a new name in the Indian tradition. In secret ceremonies only Indian names were used.

23) *Saint Tammany and the Origin of the Society of Tammany or Columbian Order in the City of New York*, opus quoted, p. 42.

24) *Washington*: an abridgment of the 7 volume opus by Douglas Southall Freeman, 1948, Charles Scribners' Sons, New York, p. 154.

25) The following are some examples of the measures taken by the Trade Board:
1699: prohibition of exportation of wool, yarn, woolen cloth from one colony to the other

1705: Pennsylvania law encouraging shoemaking industry disal lowed by the Board.
1706-8 Rejection of Virginia and Maryland laws to provide for the establishment of new towns.
1732: prohibition of export of hats
1750: prohibition of the erection of slitting or rolling mills and of

plate, forge or steel furnaces
1756: nullification of Massachusetts ordinance encouraging the production of linen.

26) *Conceived in Liberty*, Murray N. Rothbard, 1975, Arlington House Publishers, New Rochelle, N. Y., pp. 89-90. Worth quoting from the book is this passage, pp. 212-213: "The most important restrictive act of the first half of the 18th century was the Molasses Act of 1733. Since the mid 17th century, trade with the West Indies had become vital to the Northern colonies. Lacking the great staples of the South with their ready English market, (for example tobacco, rice, cotton...) the North could buy English manufactures only by selling grain and provisions to the West Indies in exchange of sugar and its molasses derivative. The North could not sell its products to England, to a large extent because the English corn laws served to exclude northern wheat, and imports of salted food were prohibited to the benefit of English producers. Boston became the great center of 'triangular trade' with the West Indies: New England merchants exchanged fish and lumber for sugar and molasses, and then traded the latter to England in exchange for English manufactures. After 1715, this triangular arrangement was further refined; the North (Newport, Boston, New York) began participating in the slave trade. Northern ships would acquire Negro slaves in West Africa, transport the slaves to the West Indies where they were in heavy demand, and then exchange them for sugar and molasses. The molasses would be processed into rum in New England distilleries, and the rum carried to West Africa to pay for the slaves. By 1750, there were sixty-three distilleries in Massachusetts and 30 in Rhode Island. And by 1771 American slave ships reached a capacity of fully one fourth of England's mighty slave fleet." Thus the North entered the slave trade by virtue of the pressure of economic monopolistic policies.

27) Richard Norton Smith has documented the nature of the exchanges between Hamilton and George Hammond, British envoy to the United States, and how these undermined the diplomatic efforts between the two countries. See: *Patriarch: George Washington*

and the New American Nation, Richard Norton Smith, 1993, Houghton Mifflin Co., Boston, New York.

28) In this regard see: *The Long Affair: Thomas Jefferson and the French Revolution: 1785-1800*, Conor Cruise O'Brien, 1998, University of Chicago Press. Jefferson's ideas about the French Revolution appear through his own words extensively quoted.

Chapter 3: Fourth of July: the Temple, the Lodge and the Longhouse

1) *Les Mysteres Templiers*, Louis Charpentier, 1967, Editions Robert Laffont, Paris, pp. 34-35.

2) *Les Templiers en Amerique*, Jacques de Mahieu, 1981, Editions Robert Laffont, Paris, p. 214.

3) *The Sword and the Grail: of the Grail and the Templars and a True Discovery of America*, Andrew Sinclair, 1992, Crown Publishers Inc., New York, pp. 27-28.

4) Ibid., pp. 29-31.

5) Ibid., pp. 12, 33, 47.

6) *The Temple and the Lodge*, Michael Baigent and Richard Leigh, 1989, Jonathan Cape, London, pp. 28-29, 64-72.

7) Ibid., pp. 96-98.

8) *The Sword and the Grail: of the Grail and the Templars and a True Discovery of America*, opus quoted, p. 5.

9) Ibid., see chapter 10: Earl and Prince of Orkney.

10) *Atlantic Crossings Before Columbus*, Frederick Pohl, 1961, Norton & Company, New York, chapter 12: Sinclair, the Sea-King.

11) *The Sword and the Grail: of the Grail and the Templars and a True Discovery of America*, opus quoted, pp. 8-11.

12) *Atlantic Crossings Before Columbus*, opus quoted, pp. 145 and 248-252.

13) Ibid., p. 146.

14) *Atlantic Crossings Before Columbus*, opus quoted, p. 20. In his short trip to America in 1524, Verrazzano spent some time in the area of modern-day Rhode Island. He describes its natives as "the most civilized in customs" and "inclining more to whiteness". This may indicate previous European settlers and consequent intermarriage with the natives. The previous explorers would have settled more than a century earlier, thereby the mixed traits of the population. See also p. 366.

15) *The Sword and the Grail: of the Grail and the Templars and a True Discovery of America*, opus quoted, p. 110.

16) Ibid., pp. 149-150.

17) *Grail Knights of North America: on the Trail of the Grail Legacy in Canada and the United States*, Michael Bradley 1998, Hounslow Press, Toronto, Oxford.

18) *The Sword and the Grail: of the Grail and the Templars and a True Discovery of America*, opus quoted, p. 108.

19) See: *The Red Record, the Wallam Olum: the Oldest Native North American History*, opus quoted, p. 129.

20) *The White Roots of Peace*, Paul A. W. Wallace 1946, University of Pennsylvania Press, Philadelphia.
Other useful retellings of the legend are the following:
The Iroquois Book of Rites, Horatio Hale, 1969, AMS Press, New York.
Parker on the Iroquois, Arthur C. Parker, 1968, Syracuse University Press.

Wilderness Messiah: the Story of Hiawatha and the Iroquois, Thomas R. Henry, 1955, Bonanza Books, New York. CHECK
Hiawatha, Founder of the Iroquois Confederacy, Nancy Bonvillain, 1992, Chelsea House Publishers, New York, Philadelphia.

21) *Hiawatha, founder of the Iroquois Confederacy*, opus quoted, p. 23.

22) *The Iroquois Book of Rites*, opus quoted.

23) *Forgotten Founders: How the American Indians Helped Shape Democracy*, Bruce E. Johansen, 1982, The Harvard Common Press, Harvard and Boston, Massachusetts.

24) *The Sword and the Grail: of the Grail and the Templars and a True Discovery of America*, opus quoted, pp.160-161, 168-169.

25) *The Temple and the Lodge*, opus quoted, pp. 115-116.

26) *The Origins of Freemasonry: Scotland's Century, 1590-1710*, David Stevenson, 1988, Cambridge University Press, pp. 8, 57, 66.

27) *The Sword and the Grail: of the Grail and the Templars and a True Discovery of America*, opus quoted, p. 168.

28) *The Origins of Freemasonry: Scotland's Century, 1590-1710*, opus quoted, pp. 19-24.

29) *The Sword and the Grail: of the Grail and the Templars and a True Discovery of America*, opus quoted, pp. 45-61. The following are some churches showing Templar and/or Freemason symbolism on tombstones: Saddel Abbey in the Mull of Kyntire, Chapel of Kilmory in the Mull of Knapdale, Cistercian Abbey in Culross (Fife), Balantrodoch (Templar headquarters), Melrose Abbey, Seton Collegiate Church, Collegiate Church at Costorphine (near Edinburgh), Douglas Chapel. A good example of an intermediate stage between Templar and Freemasonic symbols is the gravestone found in the Kilmory Chapel. In it is represented a knight; under-

neath him a Templar-style cross, above him a Masonic set square. See fig. 7 in *The Temple and the Lodge*, opus quoted.

30) *The Origins of Freemasonry: Scotland's Century, 1590-1710*, opus quoted, p. 7.

31) *The Second Messiah: Templars, the Turin Shroud and the Great Secret of Freemasonry*, Christopher Knight and Robert Lomas 1997, Element, Shaftersbury, Dorset, Boston, Melbourne, p. 11.

32) Ibid., pp. 15-18.

33) *The Temple and the Lodge*, opus quoted, p. 116.

34) Ibid., p. 211.

35) See: *I Kings, I and 2 Chronicles* and *2 Samuel.*

36) *Franklin of Philadelphia*, Esmond Wright, 1986, Belknap Press, Harvard University Press, p. 354.

37) *Benjamin Franklin*, Carl Van Doren, 1938, Penguin Books, pp. 143-146.

38) *Benjamin Franklin: His Life as He Wrote It*, edited by Esmond Wright, 1989, Harvard University Press, Cambridge, Mass., p. 102.

39) *Forgotten Founders: How the American Indians Helped Shape Democracy*, opus quoted, pp. 61-62.

40) *Ben Franklin: an Affectionate Portrait*, Nelson Beecher Keyes, 1956, Hanover House, Garden City, New York, p. 239.

41) *The Temple and the Lodge*, opus quoted, p. 255.

42) Ibid., opus quoted, chapters 17 & 18.

Chapter 4: Spiritual Movements in the 19th Century

1) *Revolutionary Brotherhood: Freemasonry and the Transformation of the American Social Order*, opus quoted, pp. 253-254.

2) From *The Other America*, Carl Stegmann, 1997, Rudolf Steiner College Press, Fair Oaks, California. See the chapter: *The American Dream* in Part I.

Chapter 5: Thanksgiving, Pocahontas and the Dream of Brotherhood

1) Most of the information about the birth of the festival and the celebrations comes from *Thanksgiving: an American Holiday, an American History*, Diana Karter Appelbaum, 1984, Facts on File Publications, New York.

2) *Conceived in Liberty*, opus quoted, Vol I, chapter 3: *The Virginia Company.*

3) Among these books, are the following:
Squanto and the First Thanksgiving, Joyce K. Kessel and Lisa Donze, 1983, Carolrhoda Books, Minneapolis.
Squanto, Friend of the Pilgrims, Clyde Robert Bulla, 1954, Scholastic Inc. New York.

4) *Conceived in Liberty*, Vol I, Chapter 3: *The Virginia Company*, opus quoted.

5) *Pocahontas: the Life and the Legend*, Frances Mossiker, 1996, Da Capo Press, New York, p. 273.

6) *The Three Worlds of Captain John Smith*, Philip L. Barbour, 1964, Houghton Mifflin Company, Boston, p. 308, and *Biographies and Legends of the New England Indians*, vol. II, Leo Bonfanti, 1993, Pride Publications, Burlington MA, p. 22.

7) *The Three Worlds of Captain John Smith*, opus quoted, p. 314.

8) Ibid., pp. 343-344.

9) Ibid., pp. 341-347.

10) Most information concerning Squanto is taken from *Biographies and Legends of the New England Indians*, opus quoted. Additional information is taken from:
Squanto, Feenie Ziner, 1988, Linnet Books, Hamden, Connecticut.

11) *Squanto*, opus quoted, notes to p. 146.

12) Most of the information concerning Pocahontas is taken from *Pocahontas: the Life and the Legend*, opus quoted.

13) It is with Reverend Whitaker that Pocahontas has the most untarnished meeting of minds. Whitaker was a Puritan and a scholar, son of a Master and Regius Professor of Divinity. He was destined to a successful career in England. His renunciation of a life of comfort and recognition indicates the depth of his vocation. It is Whitaker who encourages Rolfe to overcome his hesitations and take the step of marrying the 'barbarian' princess. Whitaker is touched by the depth of Pocahontas' acceptance of Christianity. Whether for that reason or others he recognizes of the Indians that "'They have reasonable soules and intellectuall faculties as well as wee; we all have Adam for our common parent; yea, by nature the condition of us both is all one." No little statement for the times he lived in. *Pocahontas: the Life and the Legend*, opus quoted, p. 165.

<u>Conclusion</u>: After the American Dream: the Future of the Three Holidays

1) *The Other America*, opus quoted.

touched by the depth of Pocahontas' acceptance of Christianity. Whether for that reason or others he recognizes of the Indians that "They have reasonable soules and intellectuall faculties as well as wee; we all have Adam for our common parent; yea, by nature the condition of us both is all one." No little statement for the times he lived in. Pocahontas: the Life and the Legend, opus quoted, p. 165.

Conclusion: After the American Dream: the Future of the Three Holidays

1) The Other America, opus quoted.

BIBLIOGRAPHY

Baigent, Michael: *Grail Knights of North America: on the Trail of the Grail Legacy in Canada and the United States*, 1988, Hounslow Press, Toronto, Oxford.

Baigent, Michael and Leigh, Richard: *The Temple and the Lodge*, 1989, Jonathan Cape, London.

Barbour, Philip L.: *The Three Worlds of Captain John Smith*, 1964, Houghton Mifflin Company, Boston.

Beecher Keyes, Nelson: *Ben Franklin: an Affectionate Portrait*, 1956, Hanover House, Garden City, New York.

Bonfanti, Leo - *Biographies and Legends of the New England Indians*, vol. II, 1993, Pride Publications Inc., Burlington, MA.

Bonomi, Patricia U.: *Under the Cope of Heaven: Religion, Society, and Politics in Colonial America*, 1986, Oxford University Press.

Bonvillain, Nancy: *Hiawatha, founder of the Iroquois Confederacy*, 1992, Chelsea House Publishers, New York, Philadelphia.

Brown, Joseph, Epes: *The Sacred Pipe: Black Elk's Account of the Seven Rites of the Oglala Sioux*, 1953, University of Oklahoma Press.

Bulla, Clyde, R.: *Squanto, Friend of the Pilgrims*, 1954, Scholastic Inc., New York.

Bullock, Steven, C.: *Revolutionary Brotherhood: Freemasonry and the Transformation of the American Social Order*, 1996, University of North Carolina Press, Chapel Hill and London.

Charpentier, Louis: *Les Mysteres Templiers*, 1967, Editions Robert Laffont, Paris.

Conley, Charles, C., Lindsay, George W. and Litchman, Charles H.: *Official History of the Improved Order of Red Men*, 1893, The Fraternity Publishing Co., Boston.

Denny, Sidney and Schusky, Ernest, L.: *The Ancient Splendor of Prehistoric Cahokia*, 1992, Arressico Publ., Edwardsville, Illinois.

Fell, Barry: *Atlantic Crossings Before Columbus*, 1961, W. W. Norton, New York.
America B. C.: Ancient Settlers in the New World, 1976, Pocket Books, New York.
Bronze Age America, 1982, Little, Brown and Company.

Freeman, Douglas S.: *Washington*, 1948; an abridgment of the original seven volumes, Charles Scribners' Sons, New York.

Fries, Allan G.: *Vision Quest at the Big Horn Medicine Wheel and its Date of Construction*, in Archaeoastronomy Journal, Vol. 4, Nov.- Dec. 1980.

Hale, Horatio: *The Iroquois Book of Rites*, 1969, AMS Press, New York.

Holand, Hjalmar: *Explorations in America Before Columbus*, 1958, Twayne Publishers, New York.

Johansen, Bruce, E.: *Forgotten Founders: How the American Indians Helped Shape Democracy*, 1982, The Harvard Common Press, Harvard and Boston, Massachusetts.

Karter Appelbaum, Diana: *Thanksgiving: an American Holiday, an American History*, 1984, Facts on File Publications, New York.

Kessel, Joyce, K. and Donze, Lisa: *Squanto and the First Thanksgiving*, 1983, Carolrhoda Books, Minneapolis.

Kilroe, Edwin, P.: *Saint Tammany and the Origin of the Society of Tammany or Columbian order in the City of New York*, 1913, M. B. Brown, New York.

Knight, Christopher and Lomas, Robert: *The Second Messiah: Templars, the Turin Shroud and the Great Secret of Freemasonry*, 1997, Element, Shaftersbury, Dorset, Boston, Melbourne.

Mahieu, Jacques de: *Les Templiers en Amerique*, 1981, Editions Robert Laffont, Paris.

Mc Cutchen, David: *The Red Record, the Wallam Olum: the Oldest Native North American History*, 1989, Avery Publishing Group, Garden City Park, New York.

Mc Glone, William, R.and Leonard, Phillip, M.: *Ancient Celtic America*, 1986, Panorama West Books, Fresno, CA.

Mitchill, Samuel, L.: *The Life, Exploits and Precepts of Tammany, the Famous Indian Chief*, oration delivered at Old Presbyterian_Church, New York, on May 12 1795, microfilm.

Mossiker, Frances: *Pocahontas: the Life and the Legend*, 1996, Da Capo Press, New York.

O'Brien, Conor, C.: *The Long Affair: Thomas Jefferson and the French Revolution: 1785-1800*, 1998, University of Chicago Press.

Parker, Arthur, C.: *Parker on the Iroquois*, 1968, Syracuse University Press.

Pohl, Frederick: *Atlantic Crossings Before Columbus*, 1961, Norton & Company, New York.

Robinson, Jack, H.: *Formalhaut and Cairn D at the Big Horn and Moose Mountain Medicine Wheels*, Archaeoastronomy Journal, vol. 4 of Nov.-Dec. 1980.

Rothbard, Murray, N.: *Conceived in Liberty*, 1975, Arlington House Publishers, New Rochelle, N. Y.

Sinclair, Andrew: *The Sword and the Grail: of the Grail and the Templars and a True Discovery of America*, 1992, Crown Publishers Inc., New York.

Smith, Richard, N.: *Patriarch: George Washington and the New American Nation*, 1993, Houghton Mifflin Co. Boston, New York.

Stegmann, Carl: *The Other America*, 1997, Rudolf Steiner College Press, Fair Oaks, CA.

Stevenson, David: *The Origins of Freemasonry: Scotland's Century, 1590-1710*, 1988, Cambridge University Press.

Thomas, Henry, R.: *Wilderness Messiah: the Story of Hiawatha and the Iroquois*, 1955, Bonanza Books, New York.

Tocqueville, Alexis de: *Democracy in America*, 1945, Vintage Books, New York.

Trento, Salvatore, M.: *The Search for Lost America*, 1978, Contemporary Books Inc., Chicago.

Van Doren, Carl: *Benjamin Franklin*, 1938, Penguin Books.

Wallace, Paul, A., W.: *The White Roots of Peace*, 1946, University of Pennsylvania Press, Philadelphia.

Wittry, Warren, L.: *Cahokia Woodhenge Update*, in Archaeoastronomy Journal, vol. 3 of Winter 1980.
The American Woodhenge, in The News Letter, Cranbrook Institute of Science, vol. 33, # 9, Bloomfield Hills, Michigan.

Wright, Esmond: *Franklin of Philadelphia*, 1986, Belknap Press, Harvard University Press.
Benjamin Franklin: His Life as He Wrote It, 1989, Harvard University Press, Cambridge, MA.

Ziner, Feenie: *Squanto*, 1988, Linnet Books, Hamden, CT.

Wright, Esmond: Franklin of Philadelphia, 1986, Belknap Press, Harvard University Press.
Benjamin Franklin: His Life as He Wrote It, 1989, Harvard University Press, Cambridge, MA.

Ziner, Feenie: Squanto, 1988, Linnet Books, Hamden, CT.

ISBN 1553954149
9 781553 954149